JOSEPH CAMPBELL

GARLAND REFERENCE LIBRARY
OF THE HUMANITIES
(VOL. 548)

JOSEPH CAMPBELL
An Introduction

Robert A. Segal

GARLAND PUBLISHING, INC. • NEW YORK & LONDON
1987

Library of Congress Cataloging-in-Publication Data

Segal, Robert Alan.
  Joseph Campbell.

  (Garland reference library of the humanities ;
vol. 548)
  Includes index.
  1. Campbell, Joseph, 1904–   —Contributions
in concept of myth.   2. Myth—History—20th
century.   3. Campbell, Joseph, 1904–   —
Bibliography.   I. Title.   II. Series: Garland
reference library of the humanities ; v. 548.
BL304.S44   1987   291.1′3′0924   84-45374
ISBN 0-8240-8827-1 (alk. paper)

Cover design by Alison Lew

Printed on acid-free, 250-year-life paper
Manufactured in the United States of America

To Alice

CONTENTS

PREFACE

This book is both an exposition and an assessment of the views of Joseph Campbell, who is certainly the most famous and in some circles the most esteemed living writer on myth. Yet surprisingly little has been written about him. There have been no books and only a few articles. Mostly, there have been book reviews and interviews. There have also, however, been innumerable applications of Campbell's views, usually to literary works. Many of these applications are master's and doctoral theses. Typically, they presuppose the validity of Campbell's scheme, which virtually always is the pattern in his *Hero with a Thousand Faces*, and interpret works as further cases of it.

In chapters one to seven I explicate Campbell's views book by book. I have limited myself to his major works: *The Hero with a Thousand Faces*, *The Masks of God*, *The Mythic Image*, and the *Historical Atlas of World Mythology*, only the first volume of which has so far appeared. Though I often cite them, I devote no separate chapters to Campbell's two collections of essays: *The Flight of the Wild Gander* and *Myths to Live By*. Nor do I even mention the works of the late Indologist Heinrich Zimmer, whose writings Campbell edited after Zimmer's death in 1943.

In the first seven chapters I concentrate on Campbell's interpretation of the meaning of myth. I try to answer the question, What, for Campbell, is myth saying? What is its message?

In chapters nine and ten I focus on Campbell's explanation of the origin and function of myth. Here I am trying to answer the question, Why, for Campbell, do persons create and use myths? In chapter eight I evaluate Campbell as a comparativist par excellence: as someone preoccupied with the similarities rather than the differences among myths. In chapter eleven I evaluate Campbell as a Jungian, an epithet that, rightly or wrongly, is commonly applied to him. Though I try to evaluate Campbell's views in the process of presenting them, in the conclusion I give an overall assessment of Campbell as a theorist of myth.

Throughout the book I use Campbell's own, exceedingly loose definition of myth, which includes rituals and beliefs as well as stories of all kinds. I also use his term "primitive."

The bibliography is meant to be definitive. I have tried to track down all writings both by and about Campbell. I have, however, included only published works, not any master's or doctoral theses.

I have benefited incalculably from a long series of discussions about Campbell with Timothy Hatcher, who is soon to become a Jungian analyst. I want to thank him for all his help.

ABBREVIATIONS

Campbell 1943=Commentary to *Where the Two Came to Their Father*

Campbell 1949=*The Hero with a Thousand Faces*

Campbell 1951="Bios and Mythos"

Campbell 1959=*The Masks of God: Primitive Mythology*

Campbell 1962=*The Masks of God: Oriental Mythology*

Campbell 1964=*The Masks of God: Occidental Mythology*

Campbell 1968=*The Masks of God: Creative Mythology*

Campbell 1969=*The Flight of the Wild Gander*

Campbell 1973=*Myths to Live By* (paperback edition)

Campbell 1974–*The Mythic Image*

Campbell 1983=*Historical Atlas of World Mythology*

Joseph Campbell

Chapter One

THE HERO WITH A THOUSAND FACES – I

In *The Hero with a Thousand Faces*, Joseph Campbell's first full-fledged book and still his best-known one, he has two distinct aims. First, he is trying to prove that all hero myths, if not all myths, are basically the same. Beneath the thousand faces lies a single hero, just as in his later four-volume tome a single god wears many "masks." Second, he is trying to prove that the correct approach to all hero myths is psychological on the one hand and metaphysical on the other.

ESTABLISHING THE HERO PATTERN

Campbell says that his aim in *Hero* is merely to establish the similarities, not to explain or interpret them: "The present volume is a comparative, not genetic, study. Its purpose is to show that essential parallels exist in the myths themselves ..." (1949:39n43). Here Campbell seeks to justify a comparativist approach per se, not any specific brand of comparativism such as a psychological or sociological approach. He is laying the ground for future works, in which he can proceed to explain and interpret the similarities he has established. He is opposing a particularist approach, which analyzes myths individually rather than universally.

Campbell is scarcely the first person to compare hero myths.[1] Among his many predecessors, some have likewise sought to prove merely that all hero myths fit a single pattern, not what the origin, function, or meaning of that pattern is. For example, back in 1876 there appeared a table by Johann Georg von Hahn,[2] who used fourteen cases to argue that all "Aryan" hero tales follow the same biographical scheme. In each case the hero is born illegitimately, out of the fear of the prophecy of his future greatness is abandoned by his father, is saved by animals and raised by a lowly couple, fights wars, returns home triumphant, defeats his persecutors, frees his mother, becomes king, founds cities, and dies young. Though himself a solar mythologist, Hahn here sought not to analyze but only to establish the pattern.

Writing in 1871, the anthropologist Edward Tylor[3] argued that hero myths follow a similar but less elaborate pattern. The hero is exposed at birth, is then

1

saved by other humans or animals, and grows up to become a national hero--the pattern ending here. Tylor, too, sought only to establish, not to analyze, the pattern.

Similarly, the folklorist Vladimir Propp,[4] writing in the 1920's, sought to demonstrate that Russian fairy tales conform to a common pattern, in which the hero goes off on a successful adventure and upon his return marries and gains the throne. Propp's pattern skirts both the birth and the death of the hero. Like Hahn and Tylor, Propp sought not to analyze but only to establish the pattern.[5]

Campbell's professed openness to all kinds of comparativist approaches suggests that he, too, is trying only to establish a pattern:

> Mythology has been interpreted by the modern intellect as a primitive, fumbling effort to explain the world of nature (Frazer); as a production of poetical fantasy from prehistoric times, misunderstood by succeeding ages (Müller); as a repository of allegorical instruction, to shape the individual to his group (Durkheim); as a group dream, symptomatic of archetypal urges within the depths of the human psyche (Jung) .... Mythology is all of these. (1949:382)

Indeed, Campbell, writing after World War II, argues that the establishment of the sheer similarities among myths can abet world peace. The demonstration that all peoples have the same myths will, he hopes, lead to the realization that all peoples are at heart the same. Mythic oneness may yield political oneness:

> There are of course differences between the numerous mythologies and religions of mankind, but this is a book about the similarities .... My hope is that a comparative elucidation may contribute to the perhaps not-quite-desperate cause of those forces that are working in the present world for unification, not in the name of some ecclesiastical or political empire, but in the sense of human mutual understanding. (1949:viii)

EXPLAINING AND INTERPRETING THE HERO PATTERN

Yet Campbell in fact ventures beyond demonstrating the similarities among hero myths to explaining their origin and function and, even more, interpreting their meaning. He asks not just whether hero myths are similar but why, and what their similarity means: "Why is mythology everywhere the same, beneath its varieties of costume? And what does it teach?" (1949:4)

Just as Campbell is not the first person to suggest similarities among hero myths, so he is not the first to explain or interpret them. His most prominent predecessors are Otto Rank,[6] who in 1909 gave a Freudian analysis, and Lord Raglan,[7] who in 1934 and 1936 gave a myth-ritualist one. Their analyses will be compared with Campbell's.[8]

Like Rank's, Campbell's analysis is psychological, at least in part: hero myths are the same because the mind, which creates them, is. Not just their origin or function but also their meaning is psychological: the true subject matter of hero myths is not the cosmos, society, or man's body but his mind. To analyze hero myths Campbell thus proposes using psychoanalysis, a term he uses most broadly to include Jung[9] as well as Freud:

> The old teachers knew what they were saying. Once we have learned
> to read again their symbolic language, it requires no more than the
> talent of an anthologist to let their teaching be heard. But first we
> must learn the grammar of the symbols, and as a key to this mystery I
> know of no better tool than psychoanalysis. (1949:vii)

Campbell's statement commits him to not just a psychological rather than, say, sociological approach to myth but also a symbolic rather than literal one.[10] Though any comparativist approach stresses the similarities among myths, those similarities need not be taken symbolically. Raglan, for example, takes individual heroes not as symbols of something else but only as instances of the category hero. He interprets literally, not symbolically, the deeds of each hero. Campbell's interpretation is symbolic not because it is comparative but because it is psychological: the hero symbolizes the mind.[11]

Campbell's statement commits him, further, to an initially conscious rather than unconscious interpretation of myth. He assumes that the "old teachers," who interpreted, if not invented, myths, were aware of their psychological meaning (1949:178n150), which Campbell is thereby merely recapitulating. Where for both Freud and Jung, though for opposite reasons, the meaning of myth has heretofore been unconscious and must be made conscious for the first time, for Campbell the meaning was originally conscious, somehow became unconscious, and must be made conscious again. Campbell here, as elsewhere, has a far more romantic view of ancient man than either Freud or Jung. Modern man, for him, has nothing to teach earlier man, whom he can at most only equal. Psychology, then, is either a modern technique that earlier man, directly in touch with myth, never needed or, less likely, a universal technique that earlier man himself employed.

Campbell's dual aims in *Hero* are truly distinct, and he must argue for both. On the one hand his argument for a comparativist rather than particularistic approach needs to be supplemented by an argument for a psychological rather than, say, sociological one. On the other hand his argument for a psychological approach needs to be preceded by an argument for a comparativist one.

COMPARATIVISM

What, then, is Campbell's argument for comparativism?[12] It is his delineation of the similarities themselves among myths. Campbell argues, first, that all hero myths conform to a pattern, which, adopting a term from James Joyce, he calls the "monomyth":

The standard path of the mythological adventure of the hero is a magnification of the formula represented in the rites of passage: separation-initiation-return: ... A hero ventures forth from the world of common day into a region of supernatural wonder: fabulous forces are there encountered and a decisive victory is won: the hero comes back from this mysterious adventure with the power to bestow boons on his fellow man. (1949:30)[13]

Campbell argues, second, that the universality of the pattern proves that the meaning of a myth must lie in it. The similarities are, for Campbell, too numerous to be coincidental, in which case they must have a common source, which must therefore be their true meaning. Campbell acknowledges the differences among myths but, in light of the similarities, dismisses them as secondary:

The same objection might be brought, however, against any textbook or chart of anatomy, where the physiological variations of race are disregarded in the interest of a basic general understanding of the human physique. There are of course differences between the numerous mythologies and religions of mankind, but this is a book about the similarities; and once these are understood the differences will be found to be much less great than is popularly (and politically) supposed. (1949:viii)

Campbell deems all hero myths not just similar but identical. All hero myths, if not all myths, are not just alike but ultimately one: "As we are told in the Vedas: 'Truth is one, the sages speak of it by many names' " (1949:viii).

THE PSYCHOLOGICAL MEANING OF HEROISM

For Campbell, the hero of a myth is heroic for two reasons. First, he does what no one else will or can do. Second, he does it on behalf of everyone else as well as himself. No one else dares or manages to venture forth to a strange, supernatural world, confront yet usually befriend its inhabitants, and return home to share their bounty with his fellow man:

Prometheus ascended to the heavens, stole fire from the gods, and descended. Jason sailed through the Clashing Rocks into a sea of marvels, circumvented the dragon that guarded the Golden Fleece, and returned with the fleece and the power to wrest his rightful throne from a usurper. Aeneas went down into the underworld, crossed the dreadful river of the dead, threw a sop to the three-headed watchdog Cerberus, and conversed, at last, with the shade of his dead father. All things were unfolded to him: the destiny of souls, the destiny of Rome, which he was about to found .... He returned through the ivory gate to his work in the world. (1949:30-31)

The hero may be a prince, a warrior, a saint, or a god. He can be a local hero or a universal one. The treasure he seeks can be wealth, a bride, or wisdom. He can be seeking it for only his people or for all mankind.

If literally a hero discovers a strange external world, symbolically, or psychologically, he discovers a strange internal one. Literally, the hero discovers that there is more to the world than the physical world. Symbolically, he discovers that there is more to him than his consciousness. Literally, the hero discovers the ultimate nature of the world. Symbolically, he discovers his own ultimate nature. He discovers his true identity. He discovers who he really is.

For the quasi-Freudian Erik Erikson,[14] the quest for identity is a quest for a place in society, a place expressed most concretely in a career. A hero is one who, in a changing society, forges a new place for others as well as himself. For Campbell, by contrast, the quest for identity is a quest for a place within oneself.[15] Moreover, a hero is one who discovers the place he has always had, not, like Erikson's hero, creates a new one. He discovers, not creates, a deeper side to his personality: his unconscious.

If literally Campbell's hero, like Erikson's, proceeds to serve others, symbolically he proceeds to serve himself. For symbolically he is returning not to society but to consciousness, even if the object of that consciousness, the external world, includes society. If symbolically the hero somehow still serves others, he does so by revealing to them the existence of the unconscious: theirs as well as his. If literally the "boon" he confers on them can be anything, symbolically it is knowledge.

If literally the hero is a historical or legendary figure, symbolically he is either the creator of the myth or someone moved by it.[16] Whoever invents or uses the myth to deal with his unconscious is the true hero. Yet the true hero is also every human being. For the quest Campbell's hero undertakes is one which every human being, to fulfill himself as a human being, must undertake: "The whole sense of the ubiquitous myth of the hero's passage is that it shall serve as a general pattern for men and women ..." (1949:121). Not merely all heroes collectively but every individual hero therefore symbolizes all mankind. The idiosyncrasies of each hero simply reflect the particular view of heroism of each society.

To say that every hero symbolizes all human beings is to say that he symbolizes what all humans ought to be, not what they are. For in practice few are heroic. Everyone may harbor a deeper side of himself awaiting discovery, but only a few possess the courage and perseverance to discover it. The hero is heroic exactly because he does what everyone else either will not or cannot do. Indeed, by no means does everyone even want to emulate him: "The usual person is more than content, he is even proud, to remain within the indicated bounds ..." (1949:78). The hero is heroic to those who create, tell, or hear his tale, not to others within it.

On the one hand Campbell says that the meaning of hero myths is the rediscovery of the unconscious, of which not just the hero but his fellow countrymen are otherwise unaware. Indeed, the meaning is the rediscovery of the unconscious in the mythmaker, teller, or hearer as well: they are the true heroes of the myth.

On the other hand Campbell claims, as noted, that the meaning of hero myths has until recent times been conscious--psychoanalysis being necessary to tell modern man what his forebears always knew.[17] Is Campbell thereby inconsistent? No. Surely he can consistently contend that hero myths are really about the unconscious in everyone and that all but moderns have known this fact. If he were claiming that all mankind once knew of the unconscious without myth, myth would be superfluous. But he is likely claiming that myth served earlier man the same way that it does modern man: to reveal to him the existence of the unconscious. The difference between earlier and modern man is that earlier man had teachers, or "sages," to interpret myth psychologically. Until psychoanalysis modern man has had either no teachers or ignorant ones, ones who above all interpreted myth literally.

HEROISM IN THE FIRST HALF OF LIFE

Heroism can take place in what Campbell, following Jung, calls either the first or the second half of life. Where Freud deals wholly with problems of the first half of life, Jung deals mainly with problems of the second.

The first half of life--birth, childhood, adolescence, and young adulthood-- involves the establishment of oneself as an independent person, one with a firm place in society. The attainment of independence expresses itself concretely in the securing of a job and a mate. The attainment of independence requires separation from one's parents and mastery of one's instincts. Independence of one's parents means independence of the invariably possessive, smothering aspect of all parents, who to some degree always want their children to remain dependent on them. Independence of one's parents means not the rejection of them but self-sufficiency.

Independence of one's instincts means not the rejection of them either but rather control over them. It means not the repression of instincts but the re-routing of them into socially acceptable outlets. For example, sexual desire may get displaced from one's mother or father onto other women or men. Alternatively, it may get sublimated into nonerotic love or into something impersonal like art. Similarly, aggression may get sublimated into competition. Indeed, the attainment of a mate and a job constitutes the harnessing of instincts which otherwise might vent themselves in incest and violence. When, then, Freud says that the test of happiness is the ability to work and love, he is clearly referring to the goals of the first half of life, which, to be sure, means for him the whole of life.

Because the Freudian aim is social adjustment, Freudian problems are those of external maladjustment. They involve a lingering attachment to either parents or instincts. Either to depend on one's parents for the satisfaction of instincts or to satisfy instincts in anti-social ways is to be stuck, or fixated, at childhood.

At the same time the socialization of one's instincts, if not also the break with one's parents, can never be complete. Because sexual and aggressive instincts invariably remain partly unsocialized, the Freudian goal is as much a mere truce as outright harmony between the individual and society: in return for denying his anti-social instincts, the individual gains the satisfaction of other instincts or desires--for example, for food, clothing, and shelter.[18] Indeed, a Freudian hero is one who dares to satisfy rather than deny his anti-social instincts.

By contrast, the hero for Erikson, who has a far rosier view than Freud, seeks outright harmony with society. For the satisfaction he seeks is exactly that of acceptance into society. The need for identity is the need for social identity. Where for Freud the nonheroic individual seeks to adjust to society in order to secure other satisfactions from it, for Erikson the individual, heroic or not, seeks to adjust to society as an end in itself.

Nevertheless, heroism for both Freud and Erikson falls within the first half of life: it involves relations with parents and instincts. For Jung, heroism in even the first, not to mention the second, half of life involves, in addition, relations with the unconscious. In the first half of life a Jungian hero seeks to separate himself from not only his parents and his anti-social instincts but also his unconscious.

For both Freud and Erikson, the unconscious is the product of the repression of instincts. For Jung, the unconscious is natural rather than created and includes more than repressed instincts. Independence of the unconscious therefore means more than independence of the instincts. It means the formation of consciousness. The initial object of consciousness is the external world, so that for Jung as well as for Freud and Erikson the goal of the first half of life is adjustment to the external world. For Jung, however, adjustment means not just, as for them, socialization but also consciousness. One is adjusted to the external world not only when he has secured a job and a mate but, more fundamentally, when he is conscious of the world in itself rather than filtered through the projections of the unconscious.

HEROISM IN THE SECOND HALF OF LIFE

The prime, if not sole, goal of the second half of life is likewise consciousness, but now consciousness of the unconscious rather than of the external world. One must return to the unconscious, from which one has invariably become severed. But the aim is not to sever one's ties to the external world. The aim is not regression to the state at birth. On the contrary, the aim is return in turn to the external world. The ideal is a balance between the external and the internal worlds, between ordinary consciousness and the unconscious. Indeed, one returns to the unconscious in order to raise it to consciousness. The aim is the enlargement, not the rejection, of consciousness. The aim is to supplement, not abandon, the achievements of the first half of life.

Jung assumes that in establishing himself in the external world a person has typically not wholly severed his ties to either his parents or his instincts. At the same time the pull of both has begun to fade. In establishing his independence a person has ordinarily severed his ties altogether to his unconscious, with which he must therefore be reconnected.

The attainment of the goal of the second half of life can begin whenever one reaches adulthood. It begins at no fixed age but any time after the establishment of oneself in the external world. It begins any time after one has become both socialized and conscious. Socialization as much abets consciousness as presupposes it: if adaptation to society presupposes awareness of it, adaptation to society also weans one away from the unconscious.

Just as Freudian problems involve the failure to establish oneself externally, so Jungian problems involve the failure to establish oneself internally. Freudian problems stem from excessive attachment to the world of childhood; Jungian ones, from excessive attachment to the world that one enters upon breaking free of the childhood world: the external world, social and physical alike. Either one is so fully severed from the internal world that he, like the hero's fellow denizens, is no longer even aware of it, or else one feels empty, lost, cut off--external rewards no longer providing the satisfactions they once did. One may not be aware of the source of this feeling, but feel it he does. Most "moderns," for Jung, are oblivious to the internal world. From the elite few who feel empty and therefore long for it come Jungian patients.

In psychological terms the goal of the first half of life is, for both Freud and Jung, the establishment of a strong ego. For both, a strong ego means one able to resist parents and instincts alike. Neurotics are those with egos too weak to resist either. For Jung, a strong ego is, in addition, one conscious of the external world, something that resistance to both parents and instincts at once presupposes and promotes.

The goal of the second half of life is not the weakening but the refocusing of the ego. Till now the sole object of consciousness by the ego has been the external world. Now what is misleadingly called ego, or ordinary, consciousness-- misleading because the ego remains the agent of consciousness--gets supplemented, not replaced, by consciousness of the internal world of the unconscious. That unconscious is not, again, the repressed Freudian one but the naturally unconscious Jungian one, which, for several reasons, Jung calls the collective unconscious.

Were the ego, in shifting its focus, to abandon rather than merely supplement ordinary consciousness, the result would be not mere regression but psychosis: one would have literally lost touch with everyday reality. The ego does abandon ordinary consciousness, but only temporarily. It does so only to reconnect itself to the unconscious. The real aim is to become as fully conscious as possible of both worlds. The aim is to forge a balanced relationship to both worlds.

CAMPBELL'S HERO: FREUDIAN OR JUNGIAN?

On the one hand Campbell implies that his psychological interpretation of hero myths is Freudian as well as Jungian. As cited, he declares at the outset that to unravel the "mystery" of myth he will use "psychoanalysis" (1949:vii), by which he can scarcely be excluding Freud. Indeed, he cites Freud and the Freudian Géza Róheim nearly as often as Jung.

On the other hand Campbell's interpretation of hero myths is in fact far more Jungian than Freudian, and in no small part because of the stage of life of the hero. A Freudian hero would range in age from infancy to young adulthood and would be dealing with the typical problems of those years: trying to find both a job and a mate. A Jungian hero would range in age from young adulthood to middle or even old age and would therefore be dealing with the common problems of those years: trying to find a meaning in life beyond professional and even marital fulfillment.

Though Campbell never specifies the age, occupation, or marital state of his hero, the hero is always an adult ensconced in society. He is heroic precisely because he is willing to leave the security and comfort of society for an unknown world. Campbell's hero must, then, be in the second half of life.

The hero's goal, moreover, is likewise that of the second half of life: not separation from one's roots--parental, instinctual, and unconscious--but reconnection with them, at least the unconscious ones. The unconscious, from which the hero is above all severed, is also alone capable of giving the meaning he now seeks. As Campbell describes the beginning of the journey of the second half of life:

> The first step, detachment or withdrawal, consists in a radical transfer of emphasis from the external to the internal world, ... a retreat from the desperations of the [external] waste land to the peace of the everlasting realm that is within. (1949:17)

RANK'S FREUDIAN HERO

The best way to distinguish Campbell's Jungian hero from a Freudian one is to contrast Campbell's hero pattern to the Freudian one of Otto Rank. Though Rank later broke with Freud, at the time he wrote *The Myth of the Birth of the Hero* he was an apostle.

Rank's scheme[19] covers the first half of life: from the hero's birth to his attainment of both a career and, if only unconsciously, a mate. The scheme begins with the hero's parents, who are nobility and often royalty. Because of continence, barrenness, or other impediments conception proves difficult. Either before or during pregnancy a prophecy warns the parents against the birth. If born, it usually declares, the child, who is always male, will kill his father. To circumvent the prophecy the parents abandon the child at birth. But the child is saved and raised by either animals or a lowly couple. Once grown, he knowingly or unknowingly returns to his birthplace, kills his father, and succeeds him as, usually, king.

Literally, or manifestly, the hero is a historical or legendary figure. He is heroic because he rises from obscurity to the throne. Manifestly, the hero is an innocent victim of either his parents or, ultimately, fate. True, his parents have yearned for a child and abandon him only to save the father, but they nevertheless do choose to abandon him. The child's revenge, if the parricide is even done knowingly, is therefore understandable: who would not consider killing someone who had sought to kill him?

Symbolically, or latently, the hero is no real or even legendary figure but either the creator of the myth or anyone stirred by it. The hero is heroic not because he dares to win a throne but because he dares to kill his father. Furthermore, the killing is definitely intentional, and the cause is not revenge but frustration: the father has refused to surrender his wife, who is the real object of the child's efforts.

Too horrendous to face, the true meaning of the hero myth gets covered up. The real culprit, the hero, becomes an innocent victim or at worst a justified avenger. What he seeks becomes power, not incest. Who is seeking it becomes, moreover, not the mythmaker himself but a third party, a historical or legendary figure.

The animals or lowly couple who raise the hero symbolize nothing. Invented to enable the hero to survive his abandonment, they are part of the fantasy spun by the mythmaker to make himself the victim rather than the villain.

Why the hero must usually be the son of royalty Rank never explains. Perhaps the manifest filial clash thereby becomes even more titanic: it is over power as well as revenge. Indeed, when manifestly the hero kills his father unknowingly, power provides a manifest motive.

Manifestly, the myth culminates in the hero's attainment of a throne. Latently, the hero gains a mate as well. One might, then, conclude that the myth fittingly expresses the Freudian goal of the first half of life.

In actuality, it expresses the opposite. The goal it evinces is that of childhood, not young adulthood. The wish it fulfills is not for detachment from one's parents and from one's anti-social instincts but, on the contrary, the most intense possible relationship to one's parents and the most anti-social of instincts: parricide and incest.

Independence of one's parents means not domination over them but autonomy, which indeed allows for a loving relationship to them. Seizing one's father's job and one's mother as his mate does not quite spell independence.

The mythmaker is an adult, but the Oedipal wish vented by the myth is that of a child of three to five. The myth fulfills a wish never outgrown by a biological adult. Its inventor is a neurotic: he has never mastered his Oedipal drives. He is psychologically an eternal child. Since no mere child can overpower his father, the mythmaker fantasizes being old enough to do so. In short, the myth expresses not the Freudian goal of the first half of life but the fixated goal that keeps one from fulfilling it.

On the one hand the true subject of Rank's hero myth is whoever creates it or identifies himself with it. On the other hand the true subject is every male, or at least every neurotic one. Indeed, insofar as Freud considers every male at least partly tied forever to his Oedipal yearnings, the hero is every male.

CAMPBELL'S JUNGIAN HERO

In contrast to Rank's Freudian hero stands Campbell's Jungian one.[20] Rank's hero must be the son of royal or at least distinguished parents. Campbell's need not be, though often he is. Rank's scheme begins with the hero's birth; Campbell's, with his adventure. Where Rank's scheme ends Campbell's begins: with the adult hero ensconced at home. Rank's hero must be young enough for both his father and in some cases his grandfather still to be alive and reigning. Campbell does not specify the age of his hero, but he must be no younger than the age at which Rank's hero myth therefore ends: young adulthood. He must, again, be in the second half of life.[21]

The hero's adventure begins not with any initiative of his own but with a call. Though Campbell stresses that the hero is heroic exactly because he is willing as well as able to undertake the adventure, he also says that the hero may initially undertake it either unknowingly or involuntarily, in which case there is hardly a call:

> The hero can go forth of his own volition to accomplish the adventure, as did Theseus when he arrived in his father's city, Athens, and heard the horrible story of the Minotaur; or he may be carried or sent abroad by some benign or malignant agent, as was Odysseus, driven about the Mediterranean by the winds of the angered god, Poseidon. The adventure may begin as a mere blunder .... (1949:58)

Where Rank's hero returns to his birthplace, Campbell's ventures forth to a strange, new world, a world that he has not only never visited but never even known existed:

> ... destiny has summoned the hero and transferred his spiritual center of gravity from within the pale of his society to a zone unknown. This fateful region may be variously represented: as a distant land, a forest, a kingdom underground, beneath the waves, or above the sky, a secret island, lofty mountaintop, or profound dream state; but it is always a place of strangely fluid and polymorphous beings, unimaginable torments, superhuman deeds, and impossible delight. (1949:58)

In this strange, supernatural world the hero encounters first the supreme female god and then the supreme male god. The maternal goddess is loving and caring:

> She is the paragon of all paragons of beauty, the reply to all desire, the bliss-bestowing goal of every hero's earthly and unearthly quest. She is mother, sister, mistress, bride.... For she is the incarnation of the promise of perfection; the soul's assurance that, at the conclusion of its exile in a world of organized inadequacies, the bliss that once was known will be known again: the comforting, the nourishing, the "good" mother .... (1949:110-111)

By contrast, the male god is tyrannical and merciless. He is an "ogre" (1949:126). The hero has sex with the goddess and marries her. He then kills and eats the god. Yet with both, not just the goddess, he thereby becomes mystically one.[22] He then becomes one with the world itself.

Where Rank's hero *returns* home to encounter his father and mother, Campbell's hero leaves home to encounter a male and female god, who are neither his parents nor mates. Yet the two heroes' encounters are remarkably alike: just as Rank's hero kills his father and, if often only latently, marries his mother, so Campbell's hero, in reverse order, first marries the goddess and then kills the god.

The differences, however, are even more significant. Because the goddess is not the hero's mother, sex with her does not constitute incest. Moreover, the two not only marry but become mystically one.

Despite appearances, the hero's relationship to the male god is no less positive. At the outset, to be sure, the relationship seems blatantly Oedipal: the son fears castration by the father, who in turn fears death at the hands of the son. Campbell thus cites Róheim's Freudian analysis of Australian myths and rituals of initiation:

> The native Australian mythologies teach that the first initiation rites were carried out in such a way that all the young men were killed. The ritual is thus shown to be, among other things, a dramatized expression of the Oedipal [counter]aggression [on the part] of the elder generation; and the circumcision, a mitigated castration. But the rites provide also for the cannibal, patricidal impulse of the younger, rising group of males .... (1949:139)

Róheim himself, however, departs from a Freudian interpretation. The ritual still acts out a long-simmering clash between sons and fathers over the sons' mothers, the sons still seek to kill their fathers, and in defense the fathers still seek to castrate their sons. What the sons seek is not, however, intercourse with their mothers but reunion with them. They seek to fulfill not their Oedipal desires but their infantile ones. Their fathers oppose those desires not because they want to keep their wives for themselves but because they want to break their sons of their infantile ties to their mothers. If the fathers try to sever those ties by threatening their sons with castration, they also try to sever the ties by offering themselves as a substitute for their wives. The fathers thus selflessly nourish their sons with their own blood, occasionally dying in the process:

> ... at the same time [the rites] reveal the benign self-giving aspect of the archetypal father; for during the long period of symbolical instruction, there is a time when the initiates are forced to live only on the fresh-drawn blood of the older men.... Frequently the men who give their blood faint and remain in a state of coma for an hour or more because of exhaustion. (1949:139-141)[23]

Campbell adopts Róheim's more harmonious interpretation of the clash between sons and fathers. But he carries it farther. Since Campbell's hero is in the second half of life, he is not, like Róheim's initiates, seeking an initial separation from his mother. He is seeking reintegration with her. Furthermore, he is seeking reintegration with his father as well. Indeed, he is not really fighting with his father over his mother. For, again, the two gods are neither his parents nor mates. He is seeking from the god the same love that he has just won from the goddess. To secure it he need not give up the goddess but only trust in the god and thereby surrender himself to him: "One must have a faith that the father is merciful, and then a reliance on that mercy" (1949:130). The god, as represented by the father in the initiation rite, thereby lets himself be killed by the son--much as, Campbell says later in *Masks: Primitive*, the hunted does in primitive hunting rites.

For Freud, the ritualistic killing of god is only manifestly an act of self-sacrifice. Latently, it is an act of revenge: the son is killing his father, of whom the god is a projection, for barring him from sex with his mother.[24] For Campbell, however, the latent as well as the manifest meaning of the act seems to be one of self-sacrifice. If so, then the manifest level masks no unacceptable latent one, in which case the latent level is, as for Jung, simply unknown, not, as for Rank or Freud, repressed. Even for Róheim the latent level is repressed: the infantile yearning for which "male bonding" is a substitute is repressed because it is unacceptable.

In *Hero* Campbell concentrates on the meaning rather than the origin of myth. But should he be saying that the meaning is unconscious because it is naturally so rather than because it has been repressed, his explanation would be close to Jung's. When Campbell says that the contents of the unconscious represent "all the life-potentialities that we never managed to bring to adult realization, those other portions of ourself [sic]" (1949:17), he may be saying that those "life-potentialities" are innate rather than acquired. If so, his explanation would, again, be like Jung's. He would be saying that the unconscious is unconscious not because it has been experienced and then repressed but because it has never been experienced in the first place. Rather than the product of experience, the unconscious would manifest itself in experience.

When Campbell says, as quoted, that rituals "reveal the benign self-giving aspect of the *archetypal* father" (1949:139-140), he may be using the term "archetypal" as loosely as he does the term "psychoanalysis."[25] But if not, then the meaning as well as the origin of hero myths and rituals is Jungian. For in that case the relationship between the hero and god, or the initiate and god, symbolizes not, as for Rank or Freud, that between one person and another--a son and his father--but that between one side of one's personality and another--the ego and the father archetype, one of the archetypes comprising the Jungian unconscious. Likewise the relationship in the myth between the hero and the goddess symbolizes that between the ego and the mother archetype, not that between a son and his mother.

Where Rank's mythmaker or believer fantasizes an adventure that, if enacted, would take place in the external world, Campbell's would be experiencing an adventure that, even when enacted, would be taking place in his mind. Campbell's hero would thus really be encountering not, as for Rank, parents rather than gods but parts of himself rather than entities outside himself:

> In a word: the first work of the hero is to retreat from the [external] world scene of secondary effects to those causal zones of the psyche where the difficulties really reside, and there to ... break through to the undistorted, direct experience and assimilation of what C. G. Jung called "the archetypal images." (1949:17-18)

Jung himself mentions a father archetype only occasionally and typically offers a host of disparate associations.[26] Certainly the archetype is scarcely as important as the mother archetype, which itself symbolizes the unconscious as a whole. Whatever the father archetype symbolizes, it cannot correspond to the animus archetype, which is found only in females. Indeed, even if Campbell denies the existence of female heroes--all of his heroes are male--his heroes, in encountering the father archetype, cannot therefore be encountering the animus.

On his journey the hero is manifestly discovering a new world. Latently, however, he is rediscovering an old one. The ego is returning to the unconscious, out of which it emerged but from which it has gradually become severed. It must rediscover its roots:

> ... now it appears that the perilous journey was a labor not of attainment but of reattainment, not discovery but rediscovery. The godly powers sought and dangerously won are revealed to have been within the heart of the hero all the time. (1949:39)

Having killed the god, the hero or initiate proceeds to eat him. He thereby becomes mystically one with him:

> The traditional idea of initiation combines an introduction of the candidate into the techniques, duties, and prerogatives of his vocation with a radical readjustment of his emotional relationship to the parental images.... He is the twice-born: he has become himself the father. (1949:136-137)

Rank's hero merely kills, not eats, his father--the eating being part not of the hero myth but of the totemic ritual interpreted by Freud himself. Campbell uses "myth" exceedingly loosely to include practices as well as beliefs. Morover, the eating, for Freud, is done out of greed and hatred, not respect and love: believers eat their fathers both to acquire their power and, in revenge for their sexual tyranny, to tear them apart.

Having become mystically one with the supreme two gods, Campbell's hero proceeds to become one with the whole cosmos.

NOTES

[1] For an excellent summary of attempts both to establish and to analyze hero patterns see Alan Dundes, *The Hero Pattern and the Life of Jesus*, Protocol of the Twenty-fifth Colloquy, The Center for Hermeneutical Studies in Hellenistic and Modern Culture, 12 December 1976 (Berkeley, CA: The Center for Hermeneutical

Studies in Hellenistic and Modern Culture, 1977). Reprinted in Dundes, *Interpreting Folklore* (Bloomington: Indiana University, 1980), 223-261.

2 Johann Georg von Hahn, *Sagwissenschaftliche Studien* (Jena: Mauke, 1876), 340. Hahn's chart on p. 340 is translated by Henry Wilson in John C. Dunlop, *History of Prose Fiction*, rev. Wilson (London: Bell, 1888), in an unnumbered attachment to the last page of vol. one.

3 Edward B. Tylor, *Primitive Culture,* second ed. (New York: Harper Torchbooks, 1958), I (retitled *The Origins of Culture*), 281-282.

4 Vladimir Propp, *Morphology of the Folktale*, tr. Laurence Scott, second ed. rev. and ed. Louis A. Wagner, Publications of the American Folklore Society, Bibliographical and Special Series, vol. 9; Indiana University Research Center in Anthropology, Folklore, and Linguistics Publication 10 (Austin: University of Texas, 1968).

5 Among others who seek only to establish, not to interpret, the hero pattern see Orrin E. Klapp, "The Folk Hero," *Journal of American Folklore*, 62 (January-March 1949), 17-25. Klapp stresses the variety rather than the uniformity of patterns: "conquering hero," "clever hero," "unpromising hero," "defender or deliverer," "benefactor," and "martyr." All of these patterns deal entirely with the hero's deeds, not his birth or, except in the case of the martyr, his death.

6 Otto Rank, *The Myth of the Birth of the Hero,* trs. F. Robbins and Smith Ely Jelliffe, Nervous and Mental Disease Monograph Series, no. 18 (New York: Journal of Nervous and Mental Disease, 1914). The German original appeared in 1909. All citations are from the reprint: *The Myth of the Birth of the Hero and Other Writings*, ed. Philip Freund (New York: Vintage, 1959), 3-96.

7 Lord Raglan, "The Hero of Tradition," *Folk-lore*, 45 (September 1934), 212-231; *The Hero* (London: Methuen, 1936). All citations from the book are from the reprint: *The Hero* (New York: Vintage, 1956).

8 Among others who seek to interpret, not just establish, the hero pattern see Jan de Vries, *Heroic Song and Heroic Legend*, tr. B. J. Timmer (London: Oxford University, 1963), chs. 11-12. De Vries' pattern goes all the way from the hero's birth to his death. Arguing that hero tales, which for him are about mere mortals, stem from myths, which are about gods, he suggests that heroic deeds inspire the same awe as those of gods and that by reading or reciting them one returns to the primordial, virtually sacred time in which they took place and is thereby enveloped in its atmosphere. This "payoff" is the same as that which Mircea Eliade, whom de Vries cites, ascribes to the reading, recitation, or outright re-enactment of creation myths.

[9] See, for example, Campbell 1949:255, where Campbell includes Jung among the "psychoanalysts."

[10] On the true meaning of myth as symbolic see also Campbell 1949:180-181, 236, 248-249.

[11] On the true meaning of myth as symbolic see ch. 8, pp. 97-98.

[12] On the argument for comparativism see ch. 8, pp. 95-97.

[13] Campbell (1949:10n10) takes his three-part scheme of separation, initiation, and return from Arnold van Gennep's *The Rites of Passage* (trs. Monika B. Vizedom and Gabrielle L. Caffee [Chicago: University of Chicago, 1960]). But Campbell uses that scheme very differently from Van Gennep. First, Campbell is applying to myths what Van Gennep applies to rituals. Second, where the function of the rituals for Van Gennep is social, the function of the myths for Campbell is psychological and metaphysical: the hero gets initiated not into a new social state but into a new psychological and metaphysical one. For Van Gennep, rites of passage are passages not only into new social states but also back into society. Though participants must leave their everyday places in society in order to attain their new states, they do so under the aegis of society, which not only beckons them to their new states but also escorts them back to society. For Campbell, by contrast, heroes leave society on their own, discover a higher realm outside it, return reluctantly to society, and are scorned for having left at all. When, in later works, Campbell says that the fourth of the four main functions of myth is to guide humans through the stages of life, he might seem close to Van Gennep, whose rites conduct humans through the stages of pregnancy, birth, initiation, marriage, fatherhood, change of class, and even death. But Campbell's stages, while likewise extending from birth to death, involve relations with oneself and the cosmos as much as with society. Moreover, myth exists to help the individual and only secondarily to socialize him.

[14] Erik H. Erikson, *Young Man Luther*, Austen Riggs Monograph, no. 4 (New York: Norton, 1958).

[15] It is, then, hard to grasp Campbell's distinction between the modern hero, who somehow alone undertakes an inner journey, and earlier heroes, who somehow undertook an outer one: "The center of gravity, that is to say, of the realm of mystery and danger has definitely shifted. For the primitive hunting peoples of those remotest human millenniums when the sabertooth tiger, the mammoth, and the lesser presences of the animal kingdom were the primary manifestations of what was alien ... the great human problem was to become linked psychologically to the task of sharing the wilderness with these beings.... Not the animal world, not the plant world ... but man himself is now the crucial mystery. Man is that alien presence with whom the forces of egoism must come to terms" (1949:390-391).

Heretofore the journey of *every* hero was inner--only literal-minded moderns mistaking it for an outer one.

[16] On the issue of the historicity of myth for Campbell see ch. 8, pp. 98-99.

[17] But see Campbell 1973:8-9, where he says that past as well as present "multitudes" have been oblivious to the true meaning of myth.

[18] See Sigmund Freud, *Civilization and its Discontents*, tr. and ed. James Strachey (New York: Norton, 1962), passim.

[19] See Rank's summary of his "monomyth" in Rank, 65.

[20] For Jung's interpretation of heroism in the first as well as the distinctively Jungian second half of life see C. G. Jung, "The Psychology of the Child Archetype," in his *The Archetypes and the Collective Unconscious,* The Collected Works of C. G. Jung, eds. Sir Herbert Read and others, trs. R. F. C. Hull and others, IX, part 1, first ed. (New York: Pantheon, 1959), 151-181; *Symbols of Transformation*, The Collected Works, V, first ed. (New York: Pantheon, 1956), 171-444; *Psychology and Alchemy*, The Collected Works, XII, first ed. (New York: Pantheon, 1953), 333-339; *Analytical Psychology* (New York: Vintage, 1970), 117-123. See also Joseph L. Henderson, "Ancient Myths and Modern Man," in Jung and others, *Man and His Symbols* (New York: Dell Laurel Editions, 1968), 103-125; Marie-Louise von Franz, *An Introduction to the Psychology of Fairy Tales* (New York: Spring, 1970), 41-46; M. Esther Harding, *Psychic Energy*, sec. ed. (Princeton, NJ: Princeton University, 1963), ch. 9; Jolande Jacobi, *The Way of Individuation*, tr. R. F. C. Hull (New York: Harcourt, Brace, 1967), 60-79; Jacobi, *Complex/Archetype/Symbol in the Psychology of C. G. Jung*, tr. Ralph Manheim (Princeton, NJ: Princeton University, 1967), 182-187. On Campbell's hero as Jungian see Violet de Laszlo, "The Goal in Jungian Psychotherapy," *Spring* (1952), 68-69.

[21] Campbell does briefly discuss the first half of the hero's life (1949:318-334), but it falls outside his monomyth.

[22] To be sure, Campbell, in his second, longer summary of his pattern (1949:246), makes these incidents only optional parts of the scheme.

[23] See also Campbell 1959:98-99.

[24] See Freud, *Totem and Taboo*, tr. James Strachey (New York: Norton, 1950), ch. 4.

[25] See, most notably, Campbell's apparent acceptance of Flugel's Freudian explanation of the figure of the great mother as the projection onto the world of one's relationship with his actual mother rather than, as for Jung, the reverse: the

inheritance of the great mother figure and the projection of it in turn onto one's relationship with his mother (1949:113n31). Certainly in his later *Masks* Campbell gives a Freudian-like explanation of archetypes. On the difference between Freudian and Jungian explanations of archetypes see Jung, *Symbols of Transformation*, 222, 328, 330, 417-420; *The Archetypes and the Collective Unconscious*, 161n21.

[26] On the father archetype see esp. Jung, *Freud and Psychoanalysis*, The Collected Works, IV (New York: Pantheon, 1961), 320-321, 322-323; *Symbols of Transformation*, 260-262; *The Archetypes and the Collective Unconscious*, 101-102; *Civilization in Transition,* The Collected Works, X, first ed. (New York: Pantheon, 1964), 35-36, 190; *Psychology and Alchemy*, 116-118.

Chapter Two

THE HERO WITH A THOUSAND FACES – II

THE HERO'S RETURN

Having initially managed to break free of the secure, everyday world and go off to a dangerous new one, the hero, to complete his journey, must in turn break free of the new world, in which he has by now become ensconced, and return to the everyday one. In both stages he must surmount the temptation to stay, but the temptation to stay in the dazzling new world is even stronger. Hence "numerous indeed are the heroes fabled to have taken up residence forever in the blessed isle of the unaging Goddess of Immortal Being" (1949:193). Thus Circe, Calypso, the Sirens, and the Lotus Eaters all offer Odysseus the temptation of divine, carefree, immortal life.

Though Campbell does not quite make the Jungian point explicit, the strongest temptation is the prospect of returning to one's original state: the state of absorption in the cosmos. For the "new" world in which the hero becomes ensconced is really the world out of which he, like every other entity, initially emerged. The temptation is to surrender oneself to it and thereby lose the responsibility entailed by individuality.

Psychologically, the ego, having rediscovered the unconscious, out of which it emerged, is tempted to surrender itself to it. The Jungian ideal is the establishment of a balance between the ego and the unconscious: just as the ego should not sever its ties to the unconscious, so it should not abandon itself to the unconscious. More likely, the temptation is to abandon not the ego itself, which would be only an extreme possibility, but ego, or ordinary, consciousness: consciousness of the external, everyday world. The Jungian ideal is still a balance between consciousness of the external world and consciousness of the internal one--with the ego as the subject of consciousness in both cases. For it is the ego that leaves behind the world of everyday consciousness and discovers the new world of the unconscious.

19

Even if the hero manages to break free of the new world and return to the everyday one, he must still win acceptance back home, where his countrymen are skeptical, suspicious, and resentful:

> ... he has yet to re-enter with his boon the long-forgotten atmosphere where men who are fractions imagine themselves to be complete. He has yet to confront society with his ego-shattering, life-redeeming elixir, and take the return blow of reasonable queries, hard resentment, and good people at a loss to comprehend. (1949:216)

In interpreting the hero's return, Campbell seems to be abandoning his otherwise relentlessly symbolic, psychological analysis and instead taking the myth literally. Certainly Campbell could interpret the difficulty the returning hero encounters as that experienced by the ego returning to the everyday world: having integrated itself with the world of the unconscious, the ego must reintegrate itself with the world of everyday consciousness--a world that neither knows nor cares about its unconscious counterpart. But instead Campbell interprets the problem socially: as the problem the hero faces in re-encountering other persons, not in re-encountering another part of himself. Even if the "boon" the hero bestows on others is the revelation of the unconscious within them, he is still revealing it to others, not just himself.

CAMPBELL AS MYSTIC

Yet Campbell does "psychologize" the hero's return to society as the reintegration of the now enlightened ego with the everyday world of ego consciousness to form what Jung calls the "self." As Campbell says of the hero's return, "Having died to his personal ego, he arose again established in the Self" (1949:243).

For Jung himself, however, the ego gets supplemented, not replaced, by the self. Indeed, the ego remains the center of consciousness. It is ego consciousness that gets supplemented by consciousness of the unconsciousness. Insofar as Campbell means to be a Jungian, it is, then, misleading for him to speak of the "death" of the ego.

Yet in speaking of the death of the ego, Campbell reveals that he is not a Jungian after all. He is a mystic. His interpretation remains psychological, at least for the present, but his brand of psychology is non-Jungian.

Though often misconstrued, Jung, no less than Freud, opposes unconsciousness. Both seek to make the unconscious conscious. Though they differ over the origin and content of the unconscious and therefore over its capacity to be made conscious, the ideal for both remains consciousness. The death of the ego for Jung constitutes the complete surrender of the ego to the rediscovered unconscious. But Jung opposes the abandonment of even ego consciousness:

"... the great psychic danger which is always connected with individuation, or the development of the self, lies in the identification of ego-consciousness with the self.

This produces an inflation which threatens consciousness with dissolution."[1] For Jung, the loss of ego consciousness, let alone of the ego itself, would mean the hero's utter failure, not his success: it would mean his failure to break free of the unconscious. It would mean his failure to return home.

Since Campbell elsewhere stresses the difference between the typical Oriental goal, which *is* the outright dissolution of the ego, and the Occidental one, which is its retention, he, least of all, seems to be interpreting the hero's goal as the dissolution of the ego. Taking Jung as well as Freud as representative Westerners, he says that even if Jung does not, like Freud, seek the dissolution of the unconscious, he does seek a balance between it and the ego rather than the dissolution of the ego:

> A psychological approach to the mystery of the universe ... underlies not only Hinduism, but also Jainism and Buddhism; and the fundamental insight is, firstly, that the notion of ego (*aham*) is the initial error from which all fears and desires proceed.... [E]go (*aham*) is the nuclear point of the world delusion and egolessness the first end to be attained.... My interest is in the resemblance of its psychology to the modern psychologies of Sigmund Freud and Carl G. Jung. For in these, too, the fundamental motivations of all thought and action are described as fear and desire.... Furthermore, according to both, the chief cause of mental disorder is fear and desire. The individual is enwrapt in a web of his own fear-and-desire-inspired illusions (*māyā*) .... Freud's view is epitomized in his celebrated phrase: "Where there is *id* there shall be *ego*." The meaning is, that the rational, conscious ego must become the ultimate director of each individual life--and such a view, surely, is as repulsive to the psychology of the Orient as the negative way of *neti neti* to the West. Carl G. Jung, on the other hand, represents the ideal of a running dialogue betwen the rational, self-defensive and aggressive ego, and the deeper, apparently irrational but actually superrational, superindividual forces of the inner force ....[2]

Since, furthermore, Campbell himself stresses the indispensability of the hero's return, he, least of all, seems to be interpreting the goal as the dissolution of even ego consciousness, much less of the ego itself. Indeed, he contrasts the hero as "saint," who alone does not return, to all other kinds of heroes, who do (1949: 354-356). In the saintly hero alone "the ego is burnt out" (1949:354).

Yet in fact Campbell does interpret the universal heroic goal as the dissolution of ego consciousness, if not of the ego itself. For example, in contrasting psychoanalysis to Buddhism, he dismisses the psychoanalytic goal exactly because it merely returns the patient to the troublesome everyday world of ego consciousness rather than, like the Buddhist goal, detaching him from it and even the ego altogether:

> Psychoanalysis is a technique to cure excessively suffering

individuals of the unconsciously misdirected desires and hostilities
that weave around them their private webs of unreal terrors and
ambivalent attractions; the patient released from these finds himself
able to participate with comparative satisfaction in the more
realistic fears, hostilities, erotic and religious practices, business
enterprises, wars, pastimes, and household tasks offered to him by
his particular culture. But for the one who has deliberately
undertaken the difficult and dangerous journey beyond the village
compound, these [worldly] interests, too, are to be regarded as based
on error. Therefore the aim of the religious teaching is not to cure
the individual back again to the general delusion, but to detach him
from delusion altogether .... Having surpassed the delusions of his
formerly self-assertive, self-defensive, self-concerned ego, he
knows without and within the same repose.... And he is filled with
compassion for the self-terrorized beings who live in fright of their
own nightmare. He rises, returns to them, and dwells with them as an
egoless center, through whom the principle of emptiness is made
manifest in its own simplicity. (1949:164-166)[3]

Psychoanalysis, by which Campbell usually means not just Freud but Western
psychology generally, thus fails to achieve the true goal of the hero.

But since Campbell himself insists on the hero's return to the everyday world,
can he really be spurning it? Yes, for the world to which Campbell's hero returns is
not really the everyday world. It is still ultimate reality, which pervades the
seemingly everyday one: "The Bodhisattva, however, does not abandon life.
Turning his regard from the inner sphere of thought-transcending truth ... outward
again to the phenomenal world, he perceives without the same ocean of being that
he found within" (1949:165). The hero discovers that he need never have left the
everyday world after all: "Hence separateness, withdrawal, is no longer necessary.
Wherever the hero may wander, whatever he may do, he is ever in the presence of
his own essence--for he has the perfected eye to see. There is no separateness"
(1949:386).

But then the hero's return from ultimate reality is no return at all. Not only does
he now find ultimate reality in the seemingly mundane everyday world, but he
returns to the everyday world only because he finds ultimate reality there. He would
not return if he did not. To value everyday reality only because through it one finds
ultimate reality is not, however, to value it itself. The hero's return is a sham.

Campbell's characterization of the ideal relationship between the one world and
the other is most revealing:

The two worlds, the divine and the human, can be pictured only as
distinct from each other--different as life and death, as day and
night. The hero adventures out of the land we know into darkness;
there he accomplishes his adventure, or again is simply lost to us,
imprisoned, or in danger; and his return is described as a coming back
out of that yonder zone. Nevertheless--and here is a great key to the

understanding of myth and symbol--the two kingdoms are actually one. The realm of the gods is a forgotten dimension of the world we know.... The values and distinctions that in normal life seem important disappear with the terrifying assimilation of [what is now] the self into what formerly was [to the ego] only otherness. (1949: 217)

To say that the everyday world and the new world are really one is to say that the everyday world does not exist: its distinctive "values and distinctions" are illusory. To dismiss that world as illusory is to dismiss as illusory any would-be consciousness of it. Insofar as the ego initially arises out of the unconscious to link one to that world, the ego becomes either vain or illusory itself.

By contrast, the goal, for Jung, is the supplementing rather than the dismissal of the everyday world. Jung rejects the everyday world as the only world but not as a real world. He seeks to retain the ego exactly as the indispensable link between the everyday world and the world of the unconscious. Though he seeks to integrate the two worlds, he denies that it is possible to fuse them: to do so would be to deny the reality of the everyday world. Similarly, he denies that it is possible to fuse the ego with the unconscious without dissolving the ego in the process. Campbell himself may speak of the higher state the returning hero achieves as a "self" (1949:243), but insofar as it involves the rejection of the everyday world, not to say of the ego itself, it is very different from what Jung means by the self.

There is an additional reason the hero returns, and it, too, evinces a devaluing of the everyday world: the hero returns selflessly to save others, not to complete his own salvation:

When the hero-quest has been accomplished, ... the adventurer still must return with his life-transmuting trophy. The full round, the norm of the monomyth, requires that the hero shall now begin the labor of bringing the runes of wisdom, the Golden Fleece, or his sleeping princess, back into the kingdom of humanity, where the boon may redound to the renewing of the community, the nation, the planet, or the ten thousand worlds. (1949:193)[4]

If the hero's return is selfless, the everyday world to which he is returning is worthless. Indeed, he is returning only to apprise others of the fact. Here the everyday world *is* distinct from the new one, but for exactly that reason it is no less worthless now than it is when the two worlds are one. Not coincidentally, then, Campbell's heroes include the selfless Buddha, Aeneas, Moses, and Jesus.

RAGLAN'S FRAZERIAN HERO

So obsessed is Campbell with the hero's bestowal of a "boon" (1949:30, 246) on his fellow citizens that he distinguishes a myth from a fairy tale on precisely the grounds that the triumph of a mythic hero is not merely personal (1949:37-38). For

Campbell, the mythic hero is a true savior, offering his people the knowledge that gives them salvation:

> The effect of the successful adventure of the hero is the unlocking and release again of the flow of life into the body of the world. The miracle of this flow may be represented in physical terms as a circulation of food substance, dynamically as a streaming of energy, or spiritually as a manifestation of grace. (1949:40)

One way to clarify the "salvation" provided by Campbell's hero is to contrast it to that provided by the hero of Lord Raglan's pattern.[5] Campbell's hero may literally die and get reborn, but he need not--his symbolic death as ego and rebirth as self aside. Raglan's hero, by contrast, must literally die. Campbell's hero undertakes a dangerous journey to aid his community. Raglan's hero is, in the myth, driven *from* his community and, in the accompanying ritual, is sacrificed *by* the community. Campbell's hero can be anyone. Raglan's hero must be a king.

In a scheme that goes back to James Frazer's *Golden Bough*[6] but that Raglan adopts directly from S. H. Hooke,[7] the king is killed by the community in order to insure its welfare. For Hooke, following Frazer,[8] the ritual in which the king is killed involves the enactment of the myth of the life of the god of vegetation: his death, rebirth, victory, marriage, and enthronement. The enactment by the king of the death and rebirth of the god of vegetation functions magically to effect the rebirth of crops. The enactment works by the first of Frazer's two laws of magic: that the imitation of what one wants to happen effects it. Even if divine or semi-divine, the king is not the god of vegetation himself but only his representative. He imitates, not incarnates, the god. What he does causes the god to do it in turn, and what the god of vegetation does automatically determines the course of vegetation. While the god is dead, the land is infertile. His rebirth revives the land. The function of the ritual, which is performed just before the end of winter, is to insure good crops.

For Hooke, the king is only symbolically, not literally, killed. Indeed, the king himself is not even symbolically killed. It is the god whose part he plays who literally dies--not through the effect of magic but at the hands of his enemy.[9] It is his rebirth that is magically effected.

In Raglan's version of the scheme[10] the king does not merely play the part of the god but is the god himself, though it is not clear whether, as for Frazer and Hooke, the god residing in the king is the god of vegetation in particular.[11] Because the king is the god, his death, initially literal and later symbolic, does not merely magically effect the death of whatever god it is but *is* the death of that god and therefore of what that god controls. Similarly, the rebirth of the king--or, if the king is literally killed, the birth of a successor--does not just magically induce but *is* the rebirth of the god and of what the god controls. For Raglan, as for Hooke, the myth describes the life of the god and the ritual enacts it. The function of the ritual, which is performed either at a fixed time or upon the weakening of the incumbent, is, as for Frazer and Hooke, to aid the community, which for Raglan can take the form of success in war and good health as well as food.

Going beyond both Frazer and Hooke, Raglan equates the king with a hero. For Frazer and Hooke, the king may in effect be a hero to the community, but they do not, like Raglan, label him one.

For both Raglan and Campbell, heroes are heroic because they serve their communities. For Raglan, heroes in myth serve their communities by their victories over those who threaten the people's physical welfare--Oedipus, for example, defeating the Sphinx, which is starving Thebes. Heroes in ritual, which Raglan fails to connect to hero myths, serve their communities by their sacrificial deaths. For Campbell, heroes in myth, under which he includes ritual, serve their communities by their return home with the "boon" they have secured, often secured only by defeating or at least taming monsters. Where the "boon" bestowed by Raglan's hero is entirely physical, that bestowed by Campbell's is spiritual: it is not food but knowledge. Without Raglan's hero the community would die. Without Campbell's it would be unenlightened.[12]

THE METAPHYSICAL MEANING OF HEROISM

Having interpreted hero myths psychologically, Campbell proceeds to interpret them metaphysically as well. The hero's journey, he says, takes him to not just a deeper human world but also a deeper cosmic one. He discovers an unknown part of not just himself but the cosmos itself. Moreover, just as psychologically the hero discovers not only that he has an unconscious but that his ego originated out of it, so metaphysically he discovers not only that there is an immaterial world but that the everyday, material one originated out of it:

> And so, to grasp the full value of the mythological figures that have
> come down to us, we must understand that they are not only
> symptoms of the unconscious (as indeed are all human thoughts and
> acts) but also controlled and intended statements of certain spiritual
> principles, which have remained as constant throughout the course of
> human history as the form and nervous structure of the human
> physique itself. Briefly formulated, the universal doctrine teaches
> that all the visible structures of the world--all things and beings--
> are the effects of a ubiquitous power out of which they rise, which
> supports and fills them during the period of their manifestation, and
> back into which they must ultimately dissolve. (1949:257)

So insistent is Campbell on a metaphysical as well as psychological interpretation of hero myths that he spurns those who allow for only a psychological interpretation. Thus he distinguishes between the still psychological source of the symbols used and their metaphysical meaning:

> In the published psychoanalytical literature, the dream sources of the
> symbols are analyzed, as well as their latent meanings for the
> unconscious, and the effects of their operation upon the psyche; but

the further fact that great teachers have employed them consciously
as [mere] metaphors remains unregarded .... (1949:178n150)

The ultimate meaning of hero myths is that all is one. Psychologically, not only
is there an unconscious realm beyond the conscious one, but the two realms are
really one, and consciousness will eventually return to its unconscious origins.
Metaphysically, not only is there a supernatural realm beyond the everyday one, but
again the two are really one, and the everyday realm will one day return to its
supernatural roots:

> The constriction of consciousness, to which we owe the fact that we
> see not the source of the universal power but only the phenomenal
> forms reflected from that power, turns superconsciousness [i.e., the
> primordial unconscious] into unconsciousness [i.e., the ego's
> obliviousness to the primordial unconscious] and, at the same instant
> and by the same token, creates the world. Redemption consists in the
> return to superconsciousness and therewith the dissolution of the
> world. This is the great theme and formula of the cosmogonic cycle,
> the mythical image of the world's coming to manifestation and
> subsequent return into the nonmanifest condition. Equally, the birth,
> life, and death of the individual may be regarded as a descent into
> unconsciousness [i.e., the ego's obliviousness to the primordial
> unconscious] and return. The hero is the one who, while still alive,
> knows and represents the claims of the superconsciousness which
> throughout creation is more or less unconscious [i.e., unknown to the
> ego back home]. (1949:259)[13]

Furthermore, the psychological and metaphysical realms are themselves really
one:

> The key to the modern systems of psychological interpretation
> therefore is this: the metaphysical realm=the unconscious.
> Correspondingly, the key to open the door the other way is the same
> equation in reverse: the unconscious=the metaphysical realm. "For," as
> Jesus states it, "behold, the kingdom of God is within you." (1949:259)

Indeed, *all* distinctions prove illusory: between one individual and another, one
nation and another, one race and another, one class and another, one religion and
another, one generation and another, male and female, father and mother, man and
god, good and evil, inner and outer, material and immaterial, and life and death.[14]
Again, Campbell is more mystical than Jungian: where Jung seeks only to
balance opposites, which he deems real and so incapable of being fused, Campbell
deems all opposites illusory and so seeks their fusion.
Yet the identity of at least the psychological and metaphysical realms seems
akin to Jung's notion of synchronicity: the belief that what is occurring internally,
within a person's mind, is simultaneously occurring externally, in the outside

world.[15] But in fact Campbell goes far beyond Jung, who deems synchronicity an entirely empirical phenomenon: by the outside world Jung means physical, not metaphysical, reality, and by synchronicity he means parallel, not identical, events. He refuses to speculate on the cause of the parallel, which may in fact be, as for Campbell, the identity of the two realms.

In saying that the meaning of hero myths, not to say of all myths, is metaphysical as well as psychological and that both the metaphysical and the psychological meaning is the oneness of all things, Campbell may be merely presenting or outright endorsing this view. It is never clear. At the least, he is presenting the meaning of hero myths for those who believe in them. But insofar as he says that the true meaning of hero myths is psychological and metaphysical rather than, as modern man takes it, literal and historical, Campbell is clearly presenting not just the meaning of the myths for believers but the meaning of them in fact. But he may be going farther still. He may be saying not just what the true meaning of hero myths is but that that meaning is true. He may be saying not just that hero myths really preach the oneness of all things but that all things are really one. Though Campbell never says for sure, his relentless enthusiasm for the true meaning of hero myths suggests strongly that he endorses that meaning as itself true.

NOTES

[1] C. G. Jung, "Concerning Rebirth," in his *The Archetypes and the Collective Unconscious*, The Collected Works, IX, part I, first ed. (New York: Pantheon, 1959), 145.

[2] Campbell, "Oriental Philosophy and Occidental Psychoanalysis," in *Proceedings of the IXth International Congress for the History of Religions*, Tokyo and Kyoto, August 27th-September 9th, 1958 (Tokyo: Maruzen, 1960), 492-495. See Jung's own criticism of the East for lopsidedly seeking to dissolve the ego and return to sheer unconsciousness: see his *Psychology and Religion: West and East*, The Collected Works, XI, first ed. (New York: Pantheon, 1958), part II, esp. 493. See also Harold Coward, *Jung and Eastern Thought* (Albany: State University of New York, 1985).

[3] See also Campbell 1949:89, 130, 131. In not only *Hero* but also, for example, his earlier, anticipatory commentary to Jeff King's Navaho hero myth Campbell denounces the ego as self-centered: see Campbell 1943:83.

[4] See also Campbell 1949:218.

[5] Lord Raglan, *The Hero* (New York: Vintage, 1956).

[6] James G. Frazer, *The Golden Bough*, one-vol. abridgment (London: Macmillan, 1922).

[7] S. H. Hooke, "The Myth and Ritual Pattern of the Ancient Near East," in *Myth and Ritual*, ed. Hooke (London: Oxford University, 1933), 1-14; Hooke, "Introduction," in *The Labyrinth*, ed. Hooke (London: SPCK, 1935), v-x.

[8] Frazer, ch. 29. Strictly, in this chapter, which describes his combined stage of magic and religion, Frazer does not associate the king with god. He does so only in his prior stage of sheer religion in chs. 24-26. Hooke adds the association.

[9] To be sure, for Frazer, though not for Hooke, the death of the god can be voluntary, as in Adonis' descent to the underworld.

[10] Raglan wrongly attributes to Hooke a scheme that really follows Frazer, ch. 24.

[11] It may be the sky god instead: see Raglan, *The Hero*, 201-202.

[12] On the one hand Raglan claims to be following Hooke: see *The Hero*, chs. 11-15. On the other hand he provides his own pattern: see *The Hero*, chs. 16-17; "The Hero of Tradition," *Folk-lore*, 45 (September 1934), 212-231. Insofar as he follows Hooke, the myths acted out ritually are entirely about gods, whom Raglan, going beyond Hooke, identifies with heroes. Moreover, the gods are gods of vegetation exclusively. Insofar as he follows his own pattern, myths can be about human as well as divine heroes, though Raglan argues that even heroes deemed human in myths are in fact divine. Still, he does not limit gods to gods of vegetation. For Raglan, all heroes are kings and are also gods even if within the myths in his own scheme most heroes are human--thus often losing their kingship when they lose the favor of the gods: see *The Hero*, 175. Insofar as Raglan follows Hooke, the plot of myths is the death, rebirth, victory, marriage, and enthronement of the hero/king/god. Insofar as Raglan follows his own scheme, the plot is the birth, survival, victory, marriage, enthronement, and death of the hero/king/ultimately god. Raglan fails to distinguish between Hooke's scheme and his own. He writes as if they were identical. Moreover, even where Raglan seemingly follows Hooke's scheme, he does not: where Hooke follows the scheme of Frazer, ch. 29, Raglan follows the different one of Frazer, ch. 24.

[13] See also Campbell 1949:365-378.

[14] See Campbell 1949:131, 149-192, 382-390. For Campbell, modern man above all clings to the distinctions that make him an individual: the uniqueness of his nation, race, religion, sex, class, and age. The key message of myth is therefore more telling against him than against his forebears: see Campbell 1949:385. In volume four of *The Masks of God* Campbell reverses himself and applauds, not condemns, modern individuality.

15 On synchronicity see Jung, "Synchronicity: An Acausal Connecting Principle" and "On Synchronicity" in his *The Structure and Dynamics of the Psyche*, The Collected Works, VIII, first ed. (New York: Pantheon, 1960), 417-519 and 520-531.

Chapter Three

THE MASKS OF GOD: PRIMITIVE MYTHOLOGY

In *The Masks of God*, in contrast to *The Hero with a Thousand Faces*, Campbell stresses the differences rather than the similarities among myths. He distinguishes four main categories of myths: primitive, Oriental, Occidental, and creative. By primitive mythology Campbell means the mythology of nonliterate peoples. By Oriental mythology he means the mythology of the peoples of India, Southeast Asia, China, Japan, Mesopotamia, Egypt, pre-Columbian Middle America, and Peru. By Occidental mythology he means the mythology of the religions of the Near East, or the "Levant," on the one hand--Judaism, Christianity, Islam, and Zoroastrianism--and that of native Europe on the other--Greeks, Romans, Celts, and Germans. Put another way, by the West he means Semites on the one hand and Indo-Europeans on the other. Iran is, for him, the border between East and West, though he considers Zoroastrianism Western. By creative mythology Campbell means the mythology of the modern West, which he dates from the middle of the twelfth century on.

In *Masks: Primitive* Campbell follows the explorer and ethnologist Leo Frobenius[1] in grouping all primitive peoples into hunters and planters.[2] Campbell implies that this economic difference results from a geographical and climatic one, but he never explains how. In any case this economic difference yields social and metaphysical ones, which myths express.

THE DIFFERENCES BETWEEN HUNTERS AND PLANTERS

The difference between those who eat by killing and those who eat by growing is, for Campbell, the difference between those who disrupt the cycle of nature and those who abide by it. For hunters, life ends not simply in death, itself natural, but in violent death. One either kills or gets killed. For planters, life ends naturally. Plants get picked rather than killed and die on their own at the end of their period of fertility:

Among the hunting tribes, whose life style is based on the art of killing, who live in a world of animals that kill and are killed and hardly know the organic experience of a natural death, all death is a consequence of violence and is generally ascribed not to the natural destiny of temporal beings but to magic.... For the planting folk of the fertile steppes and tropical jungles, on the other hand, death is a natural phase of life, comparable to the moment of the planting of the seed, for rebirth. (1959:125-127)

Indeed, at the next season plants are reborn, so that there is really immortality rather than death.

If Campbell were to stop here, he would be like Frazer. It is true that Frazer sees all mythology as agricultural and so makes no separate category for hunting, which he somehow subsumes under planting. But he, and following him Campbell, stresses above all the cycle of the death and rebirth of crops. Where for Frazer, however, planting is merely a practical, economic enterprise, even if it is tied to religion,[3] for Campbell it is, more deeply, a social and metaphysical one. Though Campbell says that the direct cause of the myths of hunters and planters alike is economic, the effect exceeds economics by far.

Socially, hunters, for Campbell, are individualists. They may hunt for the community, but they hunt on their own and the community is often small. Planting, by contrast, is far more of a communal activity, to which participants must cede their individuality. Moreover, hunters hunt when and where they please. Planters are bound by time and place:

This, then, is to be our first distinction between the mythologies of the hunters and those of the planters. The accent of the planting rites is on the group; that of the hunters, rather, on the individual--though even here, of course, the group does not disappear.... In such a [planting] society there is little room for individual play. There is a rigid relationship not only of the individual to his fellows, but also of village life to the calendric cycle; for the planters are intensely aware of their dependency upon the gods of the elements. One short period of too much or too little rain at the critical moment, and a whole year of labor results in famine. Whereas for the hunter-- hunter's luck is a very different thing. (1959:241, 230)

The metaphysical ramifications that Campbell infers from these economic and social ones go far beyond the point of mere ramifications, but Campbell infers them nonetheless.

THE SIMILARITIES BETWEEN HUNTERS AND PLANTERS

According to Campbell, hunters believe, first, that whatever they kill does not die. Its body dies, but its immortal essence gets reincarnated. Hunters believe, second, that their victims voluntarily sacrifice themselves--their bodies--to their killers: "The buffalo dance, properly performed, insures that the creatures slaughtered shall be giving only their bodies, not their essence, not their lives.... The hunt itself, therefore, is a rite of sacrifice ..." (1959:293).

Yet Campbell also says (1959:349) that the victims seek revenge on their killers. How revenge is compatible with self-sacrifice it is not easy to see. Perhaps Campbell means that victims seek revenge only when their sacrifice goes unappreciated.[4]

At the same time Campbell says that hunters consider themselves mystically united with their prey: "And where the animal rites are properly celebrated by the people, there is a magical, wonderful accord between the beasts and those who have to hunt them" (1959:293). How, again, unity is compatible with killing it is not easy to see. Perhaps Campbell means that only unity explains the willingness of the victims to be killed. Elsewhere Campbell explains selflessness in exactly this way.[5]

These three beliefs--in immortality, self-sacrifice, and mystical unity-- seemingly efface the very distinction Campbell draws between hunters and planters. The ramifications of hunting now seem no different from those of planting: hunters no more than planters disrupt the cycle of nature for their own selfish ends. Hunters do not really extinguish their prey, and their prey are not really victims. Rather, both hunters and hunted form a communal and, more, mystical bond. Hunters may still work individually rather than, like planters, collectively, but otherwise they prove to be agrarian at heart: they are at peace with the world rather than in conflict with it.[6]

Having argued that beneath the hunting exterior lies an agrarian soul, Campbell then seems to be reversing himself again--but now by making planters more like hunters than vice versa. Plants, he now argues, do not at death retain an immortal essence that gets reincarnated the next season but rather get absorbed by nature as a whole. Indeed, Campbell even contrasts the fate of a dead hunter, a particle of whose bone remains, to that of a dead planter, whose body, by contrast, somehow dissolves altogether. The fates of hunter and planter symbolize those of hunted and planted:

> The bone does not [like the seed] disintegrate and germinate into something else, but is the undestroyed base from which the same individual that was there before becomes magically reconstructed, to pick up life where he left it. The same man comes back; that is the point. Immortality is not thought of as a function of the group, the race, the species, but of the individual. The planter's view is [by contrast] based on a sense of group participation; the hunter's, on that sense of an immortal inhabitant within the individual .... (1959:291)

The dissolution of the planter is hard to reconcile with the purported belief in immortality and rebirth.

Still more strikingly, Campbell now contends that even if the death of plants occurs naturally, their rebirth does not. It requires sacrifices: of virgins, kings, and gods. Planters would thereby seem no different from hunters, even if in hunting the sacrifices are the food itself. In both cases others must die so that the community may live.

In fact, Campbell deems the sacrifices in planting no less voluntary than those in hunting. So devoted to the community are the victims that in Christ-like fashion they willingly give their lives to it:

> Something of this sort can be felt in the Christian myth of the killed, buried, resurrected, and eaten Jesus, whose mystery is the ritual of the altar and communion rail. But here the ultimate monstrosity of the divine drama is not stressed so much as the guilt of man in having brought it about; and we are asked to look forward to a last day, when the run of this cosmic tragedy of crime and punishment will be terminated and the kingdom of God realized on earth, as it is now in heaven. (1959:182-183)

Indeed, in planting not all of the victims are even voluntary: the death of at least gods of vegetation often comes through murder. Hence Campbell says, for example, that "East of Indonesia, Melanesia, and Australia, throughout the island-studded triangle of Polynesia ... the mythological image of the murdered divine being whose body became a food plant has been adjusted to the natural elements of an oceanic environment" (1959:190). Planting here surely seems as cold, ruthless, and self-centered as initially hunting did.

Just as Campbell on the one hand pits hunters against planters but on the other hand sees hunters as planters in disguise and vice versa, so in volumes two and three of *Masks* he on the one hand pits the West against the East but on the other hand sees the West as really the East in disguise, though not here vice versa. Indeed, he really means only to make hunters planters, not vice versa.

Moreover, the beliefs of the West, while not identical, correspond to those of hunters, and the beliefs of the East correspond to those of planters. All myths may, then, finally be one, the way all hero myths are in *Hero*.[7] The differences among groups of myths would therefore be mere "masks." There would not, to be sure, be a single plot to myths, as there is in *Hero*, but there would be a single theme or, better, set of beliefs.

Campbell associates hunting with males and planting with females:

> And the role of women [in planting] has perhaps already been greatly enhanced, both socially and symbolically; for whereas in the hunting period the chief contibutors to the sustenance of the tribes had been the men and the role of the women had been largely that of drudges, now the female's economic contributions were of first importance. She participated--perhaps even predominated--in the planting and reaping of the crops, and, as the mother of life and nourisher of life, was thought to assist the earth symbolically in its productivity. (1959:139)

Citing the Catholic ethnologist Wilhelm Schmidt (1959:318-322, 351-353), Campbell goes so far as to associate hunting with patriarchy and planting with matriarchy:

> The second stage or type of primitive society recognized by this culture-historical school of ethnology is that of the large, totemistic hunting groups .... Moreover, there is considerable emphasis placed on the role and authority of the men, both in the religious and in the political organization of the symbolically articulated community.... A very different course of development is to be traced, however, in the sphere of the tropical gardening cultures, where a third type or stage of social organization matured that was almost completely antithetical to that of the hunting peoples. For in these areas it was the women, not the men, who enjoyed the magico-religious and social advantage, they having been the ones to effect the transition from plant-collecting to plant-cultivation.... Thus they won both economic and social power and prestige, and the complex of the matriarchy took form. (1959:319-320)

In *Masks: Primitive* patriarchy thus precedes matriarchy. In *Masks: Occidental*, however, matriarchy precedes patriarchy. Campbell's views in each case may reflect his sources: in volume one of *Masks* he relies on Schmidt, who puts patriarchy first;[8] in volume three, though never cited, on J. J. Bachofen, who puts matriarchy first.

Campbell is interested in patriarchal and matriarchal societies not in themselves but as explanations of myths: patriarchy, for him, explains myths in which the chief gods are male; matriarchy, those in which the chief gods are female. When, in *Masks: Occidental*, he reverses the chronology of patriarchy and matriarchy, matriarchy explains myths that assume either the past or the present dominance of female gods; patriarchy, myths that assume either the present or the future dominance of male gods.

In equating planting with not only human but also divine matriarchy, Campbell is breaking with Frazer, whom he otherwise often follows. For Frazer, the chief god of vegetation is always male, and the king, not queen, is either his representative or his outright incarnation.[9] To be sure, the ritual enacted by the king includes marriage to the queen. Indeed, it is from their intercourse--the planting of his seed in hers--that vegetation grows. Nevertheless, the supreme god of vegetation as well as his representative or incarnation on earth is always male.

Campbell associates hunting with not only male gods in general but tricksters in particular. He also associates hunting with shamans. Both tricksters and shamans act independently of the community and even in defiance of it. Campbell here thus reverts to his initial characterization of hunters as individualists. In associating planting in turn both with gods who uphold morality and with priests,[10] he preserves his original view of planting as distinctively communal:

> The contrast between the two world views [i.e., planting and hunting]

may be seen more sharply by comparing the priest and the shaman. The priest is the socially initiated, ceremonially inducted member of a recognized religious organization, where he holds a certain rank and functions as the tenant of an office that was held by others before him, while the shaman is one who, as a consequence of a personal psychological crisis, has gained a certain power of his own.... This ambiguous, curiously fascinating character of the trickster appears to have been the chief mythological character of the paleolithic [i.e., hunting] world of story. A fool and a cruel, lecherous cheat, an epitome of the principle of disorder .... The Greek Titan, a sublimation of the image of the self-reliant, shamanistic trickster, ... is neither condemned in his intransigent defiance of Zeus nor mocked as a fool by the Greek playwright, but offered, rather, as a tragic pattern of man's relationship to the governing powers of the natural universe. Whereas the Bible, in its spirit of priestly piety, recognizing equally the tension between God and man, stands on the side of God and breaks not only man's will but the serpent's too. (1959:231, 273, 279)

THE HIERATIC CITY STATE

Planting, for Campbell, culminates in the formation of what he calls the "hieratic city state," in which the bond linking all members of the planting community gets magnified. The community, itself enlarged from village to city, becomes the earthly counterpart to a perfectly regulated cosmic order in which everything has a fixed place:

The whole city, not simply the temple area, was now conceived as an imitation on earth of the cosmic order, a sociological "middle cosmos," or mesocosm, established by priestcraft between the macrocosm of the universe and the microcosm of the individual, making visible the one essential form of all. The king was the center, as a human representative of the power made celestially manifest either in the sun or in the moon, according to the focus of the local cult; the walled city was organized architecturally in the design of a quartered circle, ... centered around the pivotal sanctum of the palace or ziggurat; ... and there was a mathematically structured calendar to regulate the seasons of the city's life according to the passages of the sun and moon among the stars--as well as a highly developed system of liturgical arts, including music, the art rendering audible to human ears the world-ordering harmony of the celestial spheres. (1959:147)[11]

The hieratic city state originated in Sumer and spread from there nearly everywhere else: to Egypt, Crete, Greece, India, China, and even Peru and Mexico.[12] Having first attributed planting myths, like hunting myths, to, presumably, the independent economic experiences of each planting society, Campbell now attributes the similarities among those myths to diffusion.

When, in subsequent volumes of *Masks*, Campbell describes the Eastern view, it involves four basic beliefs: (1) human matriarchy, (2) divine matriarchy, (3) the mystical unity of gods with humans, and (4) immortality. Planting in general embodies the first, second, and fourth of these beliefs. The hieratic city state embodies the third. It is, then, easy to see how Campbell can proceed to associate, if not outright equate, planters with the East.

If only because of Campbell's subsequent association of planters with the East and of hunters with the West, he would seem to be lauding planters and damning hunters: planters for their participation in a social and cosmic community, hunters for their self-centered individuality. Yet Campbell may in fact be doing the opposite. He may really be praising hunters and scorning planters.[13] Certainly in volume four of *Masks* he celebrates the individuality of modern Western mythology and castigates its absence in other mythologies.[14] In a separate essay he associates the mythology of the modern West with that of primitive hunters, whom he would therefore be praising.[15] But then in volumes two and three of *Masks* he seems again to be lauding the East and damning the West.

NOTES

[1] On Leo Frobenius see also Campbell 1959:15, 125-128, 171; 1962:152-154; 1964:147; 1968:574-575, 653-654; 1973:55, 57-58, 86-87; 1983:40, 78, 82, 129, 253-254. See also Janheinz Jahn, *Leo Frobenius: The Demonic Child*, tr. Reinhard Sander, Occasional Publication of the African and Afro-American Studies and Research Center, The University of Texas at Austin, no. 8 (Austin: University of Texas, 1974).

[2] On primitive hunters and planters see also Campbell 1969:120-192; 1972:30-42, 55-56, 175-178; 1983:passim; "Joseph Campbell on the Great Goddess," *Parabola*, 5 (November 1980), 75-81; "Myths from West to East," in Alexander Eliot, *Myths*, with contributions by Mircea Eliade and Campbell (New York: McGraw-Hill, 1976), 34-35.

[3] To be sure, there is planting in Frazer's prior stage of magic as well, but no myths, which presuppose the next, religious stage.

[4] See Campbell 1983:148. See also Campbell 1964:505, where he says that victims wreak vengeance when the rituals insuring their rebirth are not practiced.

[5] See above all Campbell's continual invocation of Arthur Schopenhauer to explain altruism: see, for example, Campbell 1968:71-72.

6 As Campbell elsewhere describes the ultimate similarity of hunters and planters, "Essentially, then, the informing observation supporting these two widely flung mythologies is the same. It is that life lives on life, and that without this continuing sacrifice there would be no life whatsoever on this earth. The other part of the realization is that there is a renewing principle everywhere operative that is of the nature of the earth and of the mystery of the womb, which receives seed and returns it as renewed life.... The individual is thereby united with the way of nature, centered not in self-preservation but in accord with the wonder of the whole" ("Myths from West to East," 35).

7 See Campbell 1964:74, where he subsumes Rank's hero myths under creation myths.

8 Strictly, Schmidt distinguishes three stages. The most primitive, which Campbell skips, is that of hunters, but hunters who are both male and female; the next, still primitive, is of only male hunters, whose rule constitutes patriarchy; the third is of female farmers, whose rule constitutes matriarchy: see Campbell 1959:319-321.

9 See James G. Frazer, *The Golden Bough*, one-vol. abridgment (London: Macmillan, 1922), chs. 24-26.

10 Campbell's equations of hunting with male gods, tricksters, and shamans and of planting with female gods, moral gods, and priests do not always hold: see, for example, Stephen P. Dunn, review of *Masks: Primitive, American Anthropologist*, 62 (December 1960), 1116.

11 On the hieratic city state see also Campbell 1959:143-150, 181-182, 202-203, 353; 1964:5-7; 1968:216; 1969:150-155; 1983:10; "Myths from West to East," 54-56.

12 On the spread of the hieratic city state from Sumer see Campbell 1959:148, 202, 418-460; 1962:4; 1964:6-7; 1969:153-154; 1983:10; "Myths from West to East," 56.

13 See Florence Sandler and Darrell Reeck, "The Masks of Joseph Campbell," *Religion*, 11 (January 1981), 14ff.; Philip Rieff, review of *Masks: Primitive, American Sociological Review*, 25 (December 1960), 976.

14 See ch. 6, pp. 74-75.

15 See ch. 6, p. 76.

Chapter Four

THE MASKS OF GOD: OCCIDENTAL MYTHOLOGY

Though *Masks: Occidental Mythology* appeared after *Masks: Oriental Mythology*, it is closer in spirit to the first volume of *Masks* and will therefore be considered next.

In *Masks: Occidental* Campbell argues that the differences between the myths of the West and those of the East[1] reflect differing kinds of societies. Yet Campbell never investigates any societies themselves. Rather, he analyzes the myths, which he takes for granted reflect the societies which produced them. He may continually lambaste those who read myths as history,[2] but he himself uses myths to reconstruct at least the values of the societies that created them.[3]

WESTERN MYTHOLOGY AS PATRIARCHAL

Eastern mythology, according to Campbell, reflects a matriarchal society,[4] for the chief gods are female. Western mythology reflects a patriarchal society because its chief gods are male. At the same time Eastern society is egalitarian. More precisely, it is undifferentiated into males and females, for male and female gods are somehow also mystically one. By contrast, Western society is divided and hierarchical, for male gods remain distinct from their female subordinates (1964:26-27, 254).

Eastern mythology espouses the identity not just of male with female gods but also of all gods with humans, who are therefore gods themselves. Western mythology, by contrast, maintains a rigid division not just between male and female gods but also between gods and humans, whose worst sin is to seek to become gods themselves:

But the ultimate realizations differ, according, on one hand, to those [Eastern] cults in which divinity is seen as at once immanent and transcendent, and on the other, to the orthodox [Western] Zoroastrian, Jewish, Christian, and Mohammedan liturgies, where the ontological distinction is retained between God and Man, Creator and Creature. In cults of the former type the two strengths, "outside" and "within," are finally to be recognized as identical. The savior worshiped as without, though indeed without, is at the same time one's self. "All things are Buddha things." Whereas in the great Near Eastern orthodoxies no such identity can be imagined or even credited as conceivable. The aim is not to come to a realization of one's self, here and now, as of one mystery with the Being of beings, but to know, love, and serve in this world a God who is apart .... (1964: 254)

Finally, Eastern mythology expresses the belief in immortality--a belief that stems from the assumed identity of humans with gods. Western mythology bars such a belief precisely because of its stress on the divide between humans and gods. For both mythologies, to be divine is to be immortal.

WESTERN MYTHOLOGY AS ORIGINALLY MATRIARCHAL

On the one hand Campbell says that Western mythology is patriarchal. On the other hand he argues that the West was originally matriarchal. He contends that even if archaic and classical Greece were patriarchal, primitive Greece was matriarchal. Likewise the ancient, or most ancient, Near East was matriarchal:

Jane Ellen Harrison demonstrated over half a century ago that in the field festivals and mystery cults of Greece numerous vestiges survived of a pre-Homeric mythology in which the place of honor was held, not by the male gods of the sunny Olympic pantheon, but by a goddess, darkly ominous, who might appear as one, two, three, or many, and was the mother of both the living and the dead.... Thus we perceive that in this early mythic system of the nuclear Near East--in contrast to the later, strictly patriarchal system of the Bible-- divinity could be represented as well under feminine as under masculine form .... (1964:13, 17)

More specifically, Campbell argues, for example, that the Biblical opposition to immortality represents a later, patriarchal aversion to a more ancient matriarchal belief in it:

No one familiar with the mythologies of the goddess of the primitive, ancient, and Oriental worlds can turn to the Bible without recognizing counterparts on every page, transformed, however, to render an argument contrary to the older faiths. In Eve's scene at the tree, for example, nothing is said to indicate that the serpent who appeared and spoke to her was a deity in his own right, who had been revered in the Levant for at least seven thousand years before the composition of the Book of Genesis.... The wonderful ability of the serpent to slough its skin and so renew its youth has earned for it throughout the world the character of the master of the mystery of rebirth .... (1964: 9)[5]

Indeed, Campbell argues that remnants of matriarchy exist within patriarchy:

The victory of the patriarchal deities over the earlier matriarchal ones was not as decisive in the Greco-Roman sphere as in the myths of the Old Testament .... For in Greece the patriarchal gods did not exterminate, but married, the goddesses of the land, and these succeeded ultimately in regaining influence, whereas in biblical mythology all the goddesses were exterminated--or, at least, were supposed to have been. However, as we read in every chapter of the books of Samuel and Kings, the old fertility cults continued to be honored throughout Israel, both by the people and by the majority of their rulers. (1964:28-29)[6]

Conflicts within myths between female and male gods Campbell interprets as expressions, if also justifications, of the transition from matriarchy to patriarchy. For the male gods invariably defeat the female ones:

The best-known mythic statement of this victory of the sun-god over the goddess and her spouse is the Babylonian epic of the victory of Marduk over his great-great-great-grandmother Tiamat, which appears to have been composed either in, or shortly following, the period of Hammurabi himself. (1964:75)

We have already watched [in Hesiod's *Theogony*] Olympian Zeus conquer the serpent son and consort of the goddess-mother Gaea. Let us now observe his behavior toward the numerous pretty young goddesses he met when he came, as it were, to gay Paree. Everyone has read of his mad turning of himself into bulls, serpents, swans, and showers of gold.... The particular problem faced by Zeus ... was simply that wherever the Greeks came, in every valley, every isle, and every cove, there was a local manifestation of the goddess-mother of the world whom he, as the great god of the patriarchal order, had to master in a patriarchal way. (1964:148-149)

To take two of his examples, Campbell's interpretations of the *Enuma Elish*[7] and the *Theogony* are, put mildly, strained. It is true that both myths begin with female rule and end with male rule: from Tiamat to Marduk and from Earth to Zeus. But in the *Enuma Elish*[8] it is Apsu, Tiamat's husband, who starts the conflict: he seeks to kill the younger gods because of the noise they are making. Even though their noise is disturbing his wife as well, she, as their mother, objects to the proposed solution. Discovering the scheme, the male Ea, one of the younger gods,

kills the male Apsu and imprisons his vizier, the male Mummu. Only upon the
death of Apsu does Tiamat turn against the younger gods. Even if the younger gods
are all male--they are repeatedly identified as Apsu and her "sons"--not all of the
gods on Tiamat's side are female. Notably, Kingu becomes her husband after the
death of Apsu. Even if the male Marduk, upon defeating Tiamat, rules alone, he has
defeated a combination of male and female gods. Indeed, the conflict is more
"generational" than sexual: the older gods, male and female alike, cannot stand the
noise of the younger ones.

The prime conflict in the *Theogony*[9] is even more "generational." In the *Enuma
Elish* the principal antagonists are at least mothers and sons--or, as in the case of
Marduk, grandmothers and grandsons. In the *Theogony* the principal antagonists
are fathers and sons, and the main conflict is Oedipal: fathers, fearing toppling by
their sons, try to keep their children from being born. The sons retaliate and topple
their fathers. Zeus' primary antagonist is thus his father, Cronus, not his mother,
Rhea, just as his father's prime adversary had been his father, Sky, not his mother,
Earth. There is, to be sure, sexual as well as "generational" conflict: both between
Earth and Sky and between Rhea and Cronus. But the sexual--better, matrimonial--
conflict is the consequence of the generational one: the mother sides with her
children against their father. Even if, by the end, male supremacy has replaced
female, Zeus rules not, like Marduk, alone but with many wives: the initial power
of the females, while subordinated to that of Zeus, remains. As much of a synthesis
as a revolution has occurred: male gods rule alongside female gods, not in place of
them.[10]

For Campbell, the evidence of the completeness of the triumph of the male
gods is their ability to perform the female function of birth:

> In the patriarchal cosmogonies, for example, the normal imagery of
> divine motherhood is taken over by the father, and we find such
> motifs as, in India, the World Lotus growing from the reclining [male]
> god Vishnu's navel .... Or in the Classical image of Zeus bearing Athene
> from his brain: ... as the woman gives birth from the womb, so the
> father from his brain. Creation by the power of the Word is another
> instance of such a transfer to the male womb: the mouth the vagina,
> the word the birth. (1964:157)

Likewise in Genesis God has replaced his opponent *tehom* as the creator (1964:85-
86).

At the same time female gods get reduced to not just the subordinates of males
but their evil nemeses:

> In the older mother myths and rites the light and darker aspects of
> the mixed thing that is life had been honored equally and together,
> whereas in the later, male-oriented, patriarchal myths, all that is
> good and noble was attributed to the new, heroic master gods, leaving
> to the native nature powers the character only of darkness--to
> which, also, a negative moral judgment now was added. (1964:21)

Campbell equates femininity with changelessness and passivity and masculinity with change and ambition. As he says of the gods of the *Enuma Elish*:

> In the [matriarchal] triad of Apsu, Mummu, and Tiamat ... the non-dual
> state antecedent to creation is symbolized, out of which all forms ...
> are derived. But in the new [patriarchal] mythology of the great gods
> the plane of attention has been shifted to the foreground figures of
> duality and combat, power, profit and loss, where the mind of the man
> of action normally dwells. Whereas the aim of the earlier mythology
> had been to support a state of indifference to the modalities of time
> and identification with the inhabiting non-dual mystery of all being,
> that of the new was just the opposite: to foster action in the field of
> time .... (1964:78)

Campbell goes so far as to associate masculinity with the ego itself, so that, by contrast, Eastern mythology expresses a yearning to dissolve the ego and return to the unconscious:

> In both Greece and India a dialogue had been permitted to occur
> between the two contrary orders of patriarchal and matriarchal
> thought, such as in the biblical tradition was deliberately suppressed
> in favor exclusively of the male. However, although in both Greece and
> India this interplay had been fostered, the results in the two
> provinces were not the same. In India the power of the goddess-
> mother finally prevailed to such a degree that the principle of
> masculine ego initiative was suppressed, even to the point of
> dissolving the will to individual life; whereas in Greece the
> masculine will and ego not only held their own, but prospered in a
> manner that at that time was unique in the world .... (1964:173-174)

Where the masculine goal is to break free of the mother goddess, from whom he is born, the feminine goal is to return to her:

> ... neither to the patriarchal Aryans nor to the patriarchal Semites
> belong the genial, mystic, poetic themes of the lovely world of a
> paradise neither lost nor regained but ever present in the bosom of
> the goddess-mother in whose being we have our death, as well as
> life, without fear. (1964: 54)

WESTERN HEROISM

Most strikingly, Campbell proceeds to equate masculinity with heroism. In *Hero* all heroes may be male, but they are not therefore all Western. On the contrary, they are universal. Because Campbell, in *Masks: Occidental*, equates masculinity with the West, heroism, as a distinctively male endeavor, now becomes a distinctively Western one as well:

> Hence, the early Iron Age literatures both of Aryan Greece and Rome and of the neighboring Semitic Levant are alive with variants of the conquest by a shining hero of the dark and--for one reason or another--disparaged monster of the earlier order of godhood, from whose coils some treasure was to be won: a fair land, a maid, a boon of gold, or simply freedom from the tyranny of the impugned monster itself. (1964:22)

In *Hero* heroism means less conquest than boldness: the hero is heroic not because he defeats enemies but because he ventures to an unknown land. Indeed, far from defeating its occupants, he becomes one with them. In *Masks: Occidental* heroism means conquest, of female gods above all. Where in *Hero* the hero is selfless--he returns home only to aid his countrymen--in *Masks: Occidental* the hero is self-centered--he fights only for himself.

WESTERN MYTHOLOGY AS REALLY MATRIARCHAL

On the one hand Campbell distinguishes sharply between Western and Eastern mythology. On the other hand he reduces Western mythology to an artifice, one that "masks" its true, Eastern nature. On the one hand, argues Campbell, Western mythology reflects the triumph of patriarchy over matriarchy. On the other hand, he argues, it expresses the inevitable return of matriarchy.[11]

On the one hand Campbell says, as noted, that Hesiod's *Theogony* describes the triumph of male gods, led by Zeus, over once-dominant female gods, led by Earth. On the other hand he says that the triumph is an illusion: female gods remain powerful. The Titans, whom, as the enemies of Zeus, Campbell associates with matriarchy, may one day escape from Tartarus, where they presently lie imprisoned. Even after their defeat Zeus must defeat Typhon and the Giants, both of them born to Earth. Zeus will also have to defeat the prophesied son of Metis. Earth herself remains both free and, either directly or through her present successor, Hera, in power.

In the *Gilgamesh Epic* as well, according to Campbell, female gods retain power even after their seeming defeat by male gods. The goddess Aruru gets revenge on Gilgamesh, the agent of male gods, by denying him immortality:

> "The plant is like a buckthorn," Ut-napishtim had told him. "Its thorns will tear your hands; but if your hands can pluck it, you will gain new life." At a point midway, the boat paused. Gilgamesh tied heavy stones to his feet, which drew him down into the deep. He spied the plant. It tore his hands. But he plucked it, cut away those stones, and returning to the surface, boarded, and made for shore.... But when he had landed and was on his way, he paused by a freshet for the night; and when he

went to bathe, a serpent, sniffing the fragrance of the plant, came out
of the water, took the plant, returned to its abode and, consuming it,
shed its skin. Whereat Gilgamesh--sat down and wept. And that is
why the Serpent Power of Immortal Life, which formerly was known
as a property of man, was taken away and now remains apart--in the
keep of the cursed serpent and defamed goddess, in the lost paradise
of the innocence of fear. (1964:92)

Campbell's interpretation of the *Gilgamesh Epic*[12] is as strained as his
interpretation of the *Enuma Elish* and the *Theogony*. There is no evidence from the
myth that the chief gods were once female; that even the present chief gods are
necessarily male; that there is any conflict between male and female gods; that
Gilgamesh is the representative of male gods; that the female Aruru is his enemy;
that Aruru creates his rival Enkidu for any reason other than to placate Gilgamesh's
countrymen, male and female alike; that the serpent, which steals the plant
bestowing eternal youth, is an agent or symbol of Aruru; that mankind possessed
immortality during matriarchy and that a defeated matriarchy withdrew immortality
to punish mankind when patriarchy displaced it; or that Gilgamesh individually
loses the chance for immortality as punishment by any gods. On the contrary, the
story is arguing that man is by nature mortal, has always been so, and must accept
the fact, as Gilgamesh is continually urged to do and in the end may do.
Gilgamesh's inability to remain awake for six days is meant to say that he could
never have secured immortality.

Utnapishtim, who, together with his wife, is immortal, is a solitary exception:
alone saved from the Flood because he was the favorite of Ea, he and his wife got
immortality only because Enlil felt guilty for having destroyed mankind and, in
addition, wanted sacrifices. Utnapishtim did not get immortality as a reward, and
Gilgamesh did not lose it as punishment. The gods *could* have created man
immortal but chose to make him mortal in order to preserve their superiority.
Mortality is therefore the "human condition," not simply the present one, let alone
one resulting from the revenge of spiteful fallen gods.

Campbell interprets the Garden of Eden story as a similar expression of
continuing challenges to patriarchy. Equating Eve with a female god, he maintains
that her rebellion against God represents an attempt by defeated female gods to
regain their rule--the male serpent and Adam somehow being a part of the rebellion.
Campbell does grant that this particular rebellion fails. Keeping the trio from
becoming gods themselves, God thereby re-establishes patriarchy:

Thus Yahweh cursed the woman to bring forth in pain and be subject
to her spouse--which set the seal of the patriarchy on the new age.
And he cursed, also, the man who had come to the tree and eaten of
the fruit that she presented. (1964:29)

But Campbell then argues that the earth to which Adam and Eve will, as dust,
be returning at death symbolizes the mother goddess, who, in receiving back her
children, triumphs over God. Indeed, Campbell argues that at death Adam and Eve

will again become one--Eve having emerged from Adam's rib--and thereby reunite male with female--unity being the alternative to female dominance as the triumph of matriarchy:

> But the ground, the dust, out of which the punished couple had been taken, was, of course, the goddess Earth, deprived of her anthropomorphic features, yet retaining in her elemental aspect her function of furnishing the substance into which the new spouse, Yahweh, had breathed the breath of her children's life. And they were to return to her, not to the father, in death. Out of her they had been taken, and to her they would return. Like the Titans of the older faith, Adam and Eve were thus the children of the mother-goddess Earth. They had been one at first, as Adam; then split in two, as Adam and Eve.... "The man," we read, "called his wife's name Eve, because she was the mother of all living." As the mother of all living, Eve herself, then, must be recognized as the missing anthropomorphic aspect of the mother-goddess. And Adam, therefore, must have been her son as well as spouse: for the legend of the rib is clearly a patriarchal inversion (giving preference to the male) of the earlier myth of the hero born from the goddess Earth [i.e., Eve], who returns to her to be reborn. (1964:29-30)

PATRIARCHAL AND MATRIARCHAL HEROISM

When Campbell calls Adam, an agent of Earth, a "hero," he is clearly no longer restricting heroism to patriarchy and is in this respect reverting to the universal view of *Hero*. But in characterizing Adam's heroism as that of conquest rather than adventurousness, he is retaining the view of *Masks: Occidental*: Adam is heroic because he steals what God has forbidden him to take. Campbell even types him as a quintessentially heroic slayer of monsters:

> There is an interesting use of the One Forbidden Road motif in certain primitive monster-slayer myths, where the young hero deliberately violates the taboo, which has been given to protect him, and so enters the field of one or more malignant powers, whom he overcomes, to release mankind from their oppression. One could reread the episode in the Garden from such a point of view and find that it was not God but Adam and Eve to whom we owe the great world of the realities of life. (1964:110)

In the irenic *Hero* God would be beckoning Adam to partake of the Trees of Knowledge and Life and thereby become divine himself: divinity would be the "boon" to be disseminated to the rest of mankind, should Adam have any kin.[13] In the conflict-laden *Masks: Occidental* Adam is, like Prometheus, at war with God, who opposes his quest for divinity. But Campbell, reversing himself again, makes

Adam a distinctively matriarchal hero, for, as quoted (1964:30), Adam's goal is to return to the mother goddess. True, Campbell says that the hero returns to her to be reborn, but Campbell's belief in the mystical unity of humans with the mother goddess undercuts the quest for independence which rebirth otherwise suggests:

> ... the sense of accord remained between the questing hero and the powers of the living world, who, like himself, were ultimately but transformations of the one mystery of being. Thus in the Buddha legend, as in the old Near Eastern seals, an atmosphere of substantial accord prevails at the cosmic tree, where the goddess and her serpent spouse give support to their worthy son's quest for release from the bondages of birth, disease, old age, and death. (1964:16)

Campbell's characterization of the hero's goal in *Masks: Occidental* is as contradictory as his characterization of it in *Hero*. In *Hero* the hero seemingly seeks to leave the supernatural world and return to the everyday one--the equivalent of being reborn--but in fact returns only because he finds there the supernatural world, in which case he is not really returning at all. To whatever extent the hero in *Hero* really does break free of the supernatural world, he is breaking free of the mother and thereby the equivalent in *Hero* of matriarchy. One might, then, call him a patriarchal hero. To the extent that the hero really remains bound to the supernatural world, he remains bound to the equivalent of matriarchy. In *Hero* Campbell never characterizes either possible goal as patriarchal or matriarchal because he deems the hero the ideal of every society, not just of patriarchal or matriarchal ones. But the goal is the same ambivalent one restated in *Masks: Occidental*.

WESTERN MYTHOLOGY AS REALLY MATRIARCHAL

Even if the Bible is somehow interpretable as depicting the ultimate victory of matriarchy over patriarchy--an interpretation that would be as skewed as Campbell's interpretations of other ancient texts[14]--is it also interpretable as praising rather than condemning that victory? Unless it is, is not the Bible still preaching patriarchy? There *are* interpretations of the Bible, above all by ancient Gnostics,[15] which make God an evil power and the serpent the savior of mankind. Those interpretations would support Campbell's, though even they do not make the conflict a sexual one. But they seem to be more rewritings than reinterpretations.

Aware of this difficulty, Campbell argues that the Bible does not understand its own true nature. The capacity of later Christians to extract from the story the doctrine of the "fortunate fall" proves to him that the text is really praising Adam and Eve for rebelling against a tyrannical god. The condemnation of them is only a later, patriarchal invention, which "masks" the true, pristine, matriarchal endorsement:

> ... it is certain that the ninth- and fourth-century B.C. shapers of this tale had no such adventurous thought in mind--though something

similar is implicit in the Roman Catholic idea that "the essence of the Bible story is that the Fall, the disintegration, is permitted in order that a greater good may come." (1964:110)

In *Hero*, whether or not in *Masks* as well, Campbell says that the true meaning of myth was known to all but moderns. In the light of the hoariness of the false, patriarchal reading of Genesis 3 Campbell would surely have to qualify his view.

Just as Campbell detects a matriarchal message in Genesis 3, so he detects one in Genesis 1. From the verse "God created man in his own image; ... male and female he created them" (1.27), he, like many other interpreters, infers that God himself is both male and female: "And finally, if, when made in the image of Elohim, Adam and Eve appeared together, then Elohim must have been not male alone but androgyne ..." (1964:112). Because the unity of male and female is, for Campbell, an alternative to female dominance as a form of matriarchy, the androgyny of God makes God himself a matriarchal rather than patriarchal figure.

If Campbell can show that even the Old Testament, which for him is the staunchest bastion of patriarchy, itself sanctions matriarchy, then he can show that matriarchy is truly panhuman and that all mythology, which reflects society, is therefore at heart matriarchal as well.[16]

WESTERN AND HUNTING MYTHOLOGIES, EASTERN AND PLANTING ONES

It is not clear whether Campbell is equating Western mythology with that of primitive hunting and Eastern mythology with that of primitive planting. Seemingly, the pairs are distinct. First of all, hunting and planting mythologies are those of nonliterate cultures. Western and Eastern mythologies are those of literate ones. Second, hunting and planting mythologies are tied to economics. Western and Eastern mythologies are autonomous.

Still, the beliefs of hunting and planting mythologies are at least close to those of Western and Eastern mythologies. Campbell associates both hunting and Western mythologies with patriarchy, divine and human alike. Because he does not link Western and Eastern mythologies to economics, he does not link Western mythology to a male occupation, the way he considers hunting a male preserve. But he does associate both mythologies with politics: males rule both in heaven and on earth. Similarly, Campbell associates planting and Eastern mythologies with matriarchy, divine and human alike. Even if he does not associate Eastern mythology with planting, he does deem the chief gods of both mythologies gods of earth and fertility (1964:22, 26, 29).

Furthermore, Campbell associates both hunting and Western mythologies with aggression and both planting and Eastern mythologies with peace. Where hunters kill for food, planters grow theirs. Though again Campbell draws no economic parallels, he does say analogously that where patriarchy in Western mythology requires the violent toppling of an original matriarchy, Eastern matriarchy, while fighting back, rules peacefully during its tenure. Since in *Masks: Primitive*

Campbell considers patriarchy an earlier and not, as in *Masks: Occidental*, a later stage than matriarchy,[17] he does not there appeal to the means of its emergence as an argument for its link to violence.

Campbell also links both hunting and Western mythologies to self-centeredness and individuality and both planting and Eastern mythologies to selflessness and community. Where hunters hunt individually, planters plant in a group. Where the Western hero fights only for himself, the Eastern one, if there is one, fights for others.

Where hunters and hunted stand pitted against each other--one distinction among many that Campbell then severely qualifies--planters and planted are part of a single community. There is a mystical bond not just between planters and planted but also between them and the sacrifices offered by planters to spur the growth of plants--a bond that, to be sure, Campbell in turn attributes to hunters and hunted as well. Where in Western mythology male gods stand above not only female gods but also all humans, in Eastern mythology female gods are mystically one with not only male gods but also humans. Confining himself to the relations between primitives and the sources of their food, Campbell does not discuss the relations between primitives and gods. Whether it is possible to extrapolate from the one to the other it is hard to say, in which case it is hard to say whether the beliefs of hunting and planting mythologies truly match those of Western and Eastern ones.

Finally, Campbell associates hunting and Western mythologies with mortality and planting and Eastern mythologies with immortality. Where the hunted dies, the planted is annually reborn--further distinctions that, to be sure, Campbell then qualifies if not virtually denies. Where in Western mythology humans are distinct from gods and are therefore mortal, in Eastern mythology they are gods themselves and are therefore immortal. Because, again, Campbell concentrates on the relations between primitives and the sources of their food, he deals with the longevity of those sources themselves, not of humans. Whether it is possible to extrapolate from the longevity of those sources to that of humans themselves it is hard to say. In that case it is, again, hard to say whether the beliefs of hunting and planting mythologies truly parallel those of Western and Eastern ones. If they do, and if Campbell is saying that planters are really hunters and Westerners really Easterners, and if, in addition, he is saying that what he calls "creative mythology" is really only a revival of primitive hunting mythology, then he is indeed saying in *Masks* that all mythology is one.

One assertion that Campbell makes at the outset of *Masks: Occidental* does identify the East with primitive planting, whether or not it identifies the West with primitive hunting. On the one hand he says that primitive planting culminated in the "hieratic city state" of Sumer, from which it spread to both the West and the East. On the other hand the subsequent difference, for him, between the West and the East is the invasion in the West by two groups: Aryans, a branch of Indo-Europeans (1964:7), and Semites--Sumerians being non-Semitic. Their dual conquest established the two main subgroups within the West: the European and what Campbell archaically calls the "Levantine." The European strain is composed of Greeks, Romans, Celts, and Germans (1964:4); the Levantine, of Jews, Christians, Muslims, and Zoroastrians.

By contrast, the East, for Campbell, remained untouched. It has therby preserved virtually intact the outlook of the hieratic city state:

> Nothing quite of the kind has ever seriously troubled the mentality of the Orient east of Iran, where the old hieratic Bronze Age cosmology of the ever-circling eons--static yet turning ever, in a round of mathematical impersonality, from everlasting to everlasting-- endures to this day as the last word on the universe and the place of man within it.... [T]his Bronze Age image of the cosmos, still intact in the Orient, renders a fixed world of fixed duties, roles, and possibilities: not a process, but a state; and the individual, whether man or god, is but a flash among the facets. (1964:5-6)

Here, at least, Campbell is explicitly equating the East with planting, whether or not the West with hunting.

Yet Campbell then typically argues that the planting outlook was never really extinguished by the Semitic and Aryan conquerers of the Near East and Europe. Rather, the Westerners were themselves assimilated,[18] so that, consciously or unconsciously, the planting, which is to say Eastern, outlook remained. In that case the Eastern outlook proves universal--save for any surviving descendants of primitive hunters.

CAMPBELL AND BACHOFEN ON MATRIARCHY

Campbell's distinction between Eastern and Western mythology derives ultimately from the classic distinction first drawn by the nineteenth-century Swiss classicist and jurist J. J. Bachofen. Though Campbell oddly never mentions Bachofen in *Masks*, he does write the introduction to a translation of his writings.[19] In *Mutterrecht* and other works Bachofen argues that prior to the present state of patriarchy, which has existed for so long as to seem natural, there was a state of matriarchy, or "mother right"--a term Campbell uses in *Masks* (1964:22, 34) but never attributes to Bachofen. Like Campbell, Bachofen associates matriarchy with the East and patriarchy with the West. For Bachofen, matriarchy existed in not only Asia and Africa but also the Near East and Greece until the emergence of Israel on the one hand and Athens on the other. Patriarchy began in classical Greece and established itself firmly in Rome, from which it spread elsewhere.[20]

Bachofen characterizes matriarchy and patriarchy in ways comparable with Campbell's. In matriarchy the chief gods are female; in patriarchy, male. Though Bachofen stresses the point far more, for him, as for Campbell, female gods are earth gods and male gods sky and sun gods. For Bachofen, Demeter is the quintessential matriarchal god and Apollo the quintessential patriarchal god.

For Bachofen, as for Campbell, the prime matriarchal values are changelessness, passivity, peace, selflessness, and equality: if matriarchy means female dominance, it also means, as for Campbell, the equality of males and females. Campbell carries equality farther than Bachofen to outright unity, and the unity of humans with gods as well as of male with female gods. In turn, Bachofen carries selflessness farther than Campbell to universal love. For both, the prime patriarchal values are change, activity, ambition, fighting, self-centeredness, and hierarchy, which means the subordination of both females to males and humans to gods. Bachofen equates self-centeredness with nationalism. In *Hero* Campbell argues that myth preaches universalism rather than nationalism, but he does not equate nationalism with patriarchy. For Bachofen, as for Campbell in *Masks: Occidental*, not *Hero*, hero myths are distinctively patriarchal: they applaud the grandest strivings of their always male protagonists. Where, as noted, Campbell allows for matriarchal heroes, those heroes seek only to return to the pristine state of unity with the mother goddess.

There are, however, considerable differences between Bachofen and Campbell. Bachofen is interested in the matriarchal and patriarchal societies that produced their accompanying myths. Campbell, while assuming that the myths reflect the societies that produced them,[21] is far more interested in the myths themselves. Hence he is not at all, like Bachofen, interested in matriarchal and patriarchal institutions--for example, those of inheritance and law. Campbell views matriarchy and patriarchy as less political than psychological entities: they represent aspects of all humans. Matriarchy, for him, means the primacy of the female side in all humans; patriarchy, the primacy of the male.

Like Campbell in *Masks: Primitive*, Bachofen associates matriarchy with planting,[22] but he does not, like Campbell, also associate patriarchy with hunting. Rather, he associates hunting, together with gathering, with a third stage, one earlier than either matriarchy or patriarchy.[23] Here males rule females, but there is no notion of paternity and so of male descent. There is no concept of property either and so no notion of male inheritance. Above all, there is no concept of family and so of marriage. There is promiscuity: females are collectively available to males.

Because even matriarchy does not, for Bachofen, espouse the outright unity of male gods with female ones or of humans with gods, matriarchy is far less mystical than it is for Campbell. Matriarchy espouses universal love but not identity. Hence it does not, for example, preach human immortality, which would mean divinity. For both Bachofen and Campbell, however, patriarchy does mean division and opposition among all things.

For Bachofen, the succession of matriarchy by patriarchy means merely the succession of female dominance by male. For Campbell, it can, in extreme cases, mean more: the virtual replacement of females by males. In a reversal of "Amazonianism," which Bachofen himself deems an extreme case of the shift from his first stage to matriarchy, males, for Campbell, replace females by giving birth themselves. For Bachofen, by contrast, females in patriarchy continue to give birth. Only the line of descent and inheritance changes.

At the same time Bachofen deems the shift from matriarchy to patriarchy a real one, not, as for Campbell, a superficial one. For Campbell, matriarchy alone fits the true, matriarchal nature of man. Even if there have been patriarchal societies, which patriarchal myths reflect, they have been artificial departures from the essentially matriarchal character of males and females alike. The attempt to deny that character is vain, so that Campbell, unlike Bachofen, is concerned to show myths in which matriarchy finally triumphs. Where for Campbell patriarchy only seemingly triumphs, for Bachofen it actually does. For example, Bachofen interprets the *Oresteia*[24] as a depiction of the actual triumph of patriarchy over matriarchy: Apollo, Athena, and ultimately Zeus vanquish the Furies, who, if placated, nevertheless cede their matriarchal revenge. By contrast, Campbell would surely interpret the place accorded the Furies as evidence of their ultimate triumph.

For Campbell, matriarchy is not only the sole stage but the ideal one. It alone fulfills human nature. For Bachofen, by contrast, matriarchy is neither the sole stage nor even the ideal one. For all of Bachofen's undeniable yearning for the lost matriarchal age, he deems patriarchy higher. Patriarchy represents the elevation of spirit over matter, of reason over emotion, and of striving over passivity. Bachofen does object to the onesidedness of sheer patriarchy and, in a further complication, does see moderate, non-Amazonian matriarchy as an ideal balance of patriarchal and matriarchal values. But he nevertheless somehow still considers patriarchy superior.[25]

NOTES

[1] On the differences between the West and the East see, in addition to *Masks*, Campbell 1969:195-207; 1973:chs. 4, 5; "The Occult in Myth and Literature," in *Literature and the Occult*, ed. Luanne Frank (Arlington: University of Texas at Arlington, 1977), 4-12.

[2] See ch. 8, pp. 98-99.

[3] In her review of not *Masks* but the *Historical Atlas of World Mythology* Wendy O'Flaherty (*New York Times Book Review* [December 18, 1983], 24) makes the same criticism.

[4] Yet in his essay "Joseph Campbell on the Great Goddess" (*Parabola*, 5 [November 1980], 77) Campbell declares, most surprisingly, that while through planting "the prestige of women in the villages became enlarged," he "doubts" that "there was ever anything on earth like a matriarchy ...."

[5] See also Campbell 1964:16.

[6] See also Campbell 1964:86.

[7] On the *Enuma Elish* see also Campbell, "Joseph Campbell on the Great Goddess," *Parabola*, 5 (November 1980), 81-82.

[8] See "The Creation Myth," tr. E. A. Speiser, in *Ancient Near Eastern Texts*, ed. James B. Pritchard, third ed. (Princeton, NJ: Princeton University, 1969), 60-72.

[9] See Hesiod, *Theogony*, tr. Richmond Lattimore, in *Hesiod*, ed. and tr. Lattimore (Ann Arbor: University of Michigan, 1959), 119-186.

[10] Campbell himself does note female co-rule but interprets it as the return of the initially defeated females rather than as evidence of the absence of conflict in the first place: see below, p. 43.

[11] On the return of female gods, if not here of matriarchy itself, see Campbell, "Joseph Campbell on the Great Goddess," 82-84.

[12] See "The Epic of Gilgamesh," tr. E. A. Speiser, in *Ancient Near Eastern Texts*, ed. Pritchard, 72-99.

[13] Campbell does cite an earlier Near Eastern version of an irenic, Adam-like myth: see Campbell 1964:13-14.

[14] Since both Adam and the serpent are male, can the rebellion by them and Eve against God, who is, to be sure, male, really be taken as a sexual conflict rather than, like the one in the *Gilgamesh Epic*, as a conflict between humans and God-- with the serpent perhaps constituting a rival deity?

[15] See, for example, Hans Jonas, *The Gnostic Religion*, second ed. (Boston: Beacon, 1963), 92-94.

[16] See also Campbell, "Joseph Campbell on the Great Goddess," 83-84.

[17] In "Joseph Campbell on the Great Goddess" (75-82) Campbell in effect resolves this seeming inconsistency by arguing for three stages: first, that of primitive hunters, who are patriarchal; next, that of both primitive planters and their Eastern descendants--both being matriarchal; and then that of Western warriors. In *Masks: Occidental*, as already quoted (1964:5-6), Campbell says that the East continues the tradition of primitive planters, but only in "Joseph Campbell on the Great Goddess" does he in effect fuse the two stages into one.

[18] But in "Joseph Campbell on the Great Goddess" (82-84) Campbell says that the Semitic tradition differed from its Indo-European counterpart in resisting the assimilation.

[19] Campbell, introduction to *Myth, Religion, and Mother Right: Selected Writings of J. J. Bachofen*, tr. Ralph Manheim (Princeton, NJ: Princeton University, 1967), xxv-lvii. Campbell also mentions Bachofen in his introduction to Helen Diner, *Mother and Amazons*, ed. and tr. John Philip Lundin (New York: Julian, 1965), vii-ix.

[20] For summaries of the assessment and influence of Bachofen's speculations see Robert H. Lowie, *The History of Ethnological Theory* (New York: Rinehart, 1937), 40-43; Sol Tax, "From Lafitau to Radcliffe-Brown: A Short History of the Study of Social Organization," in *Social Anthropology of North American Tribes*, ed. Fred Eggan, enlarged ed. (Chicago: University of Chicago, 1955), 452-456; George W. Stocking, Jr., review of Bachofen, *Myth, Religion, and Mother Right*, *American Anthropologist*, 70 (December 1968), 1188-1190; Jonathan D. Fishbane, "The Bachofen Literature: the Problem of Interpretation," *Annals of Scholarship*, 3 (n. d.), 77-101.

[21] But note again Campbell's remarks in note 4.

[22] Bachofen, *Myth, Religion, and Mother Right*, 92.

[23] *Ibid.*, 93-100.

[24] *Ibid.*, 158-165.

[25] For an updated version of Bachofen's notion of a pre-patriarchal matriarchy see Erich Fromm, "The Oedipus Myth," *Scientific American*, 180 (January 1949), 22-27; Fromm, *The Crisis of Psychoanalysis* (Greenwich, CT: Fawcett, 1970), chs. 6-7; Fromm, *Greatness and Limitations of Freud's Thought* (New York: Mentor, 1981), 29-36. Fromm cites Bachofen but turns his ethereal clash into a more mundane political and social one: the clash is now over power, not values.

Chapter Five

THE MASKS OF GOD: ORIENTAL MYTHOLOGY

In *Masks: Oriental,* in contrast to *Masks: Occidental,* Campbell does not proceed to deny the differences he enumerates between the West and the East. He does grant that there are exceptions to the distinctions,[1] but he does not thereby deny the distinctions themselves. As he bluntly puts it, "Two completely opposed mythologies ... have come together in the modern world" (1962:9).

Campbell makes the same basic distinctions in *Masks: Oriental* as in *Masks: Occidental,* but his emphases are different. In *Masks: Occidental* the fundamental difference between West and East is the difference between patriarchy and matriarchy. From this difference, which for Campbell is one more of values than of form of society, Campbell derives all the other differences:

(1) the stress in the West on the domination of male gods over female gods and of gods over humans; the stress in the East on the equality of all gods and of gods with humans;

(2) hierarchy aside, the stress in the West on the distinction between male and female gods and between gods and humans; the stress in the East on the mystical oneness of all of them;

(3) the emphasis in the West on human mortality; the emphasis in the East on immortality;

(4) the stress in the West on ambition and aggression; the stress in the East on passivity and peace;

(5) the commitment in the West to heroism; the indifference to it in the East, at least when heroism takes the form of ambition and striving; and

(6) in psychological terms, the desire in the West to develop a strong, independent ego; the desire in the East to dissolve the ego and regress to sheer unconsciousness.

In *Masks: Oriental* Campbell gives much less emphasis to the difference between Western patriarchy and Eastern matriarchy. Though he does contrast the Western division into male and female to the Eastern unification of the two, he contrasts far more the Western division into divine and human to the Eastern unification of them. Moreover, he ascribes this difference not to patriarchy and matriarchy but to the stress in the West on distinctions and in the East on the dissolution of them. From this fundamental difference come all others, including the difference between patriarchy and matriarchy.

DIFFERENCES IN THE CONCEPT OF TIME

The West, according to Campbell, makes distinctions of all kinds. Temporally, it distinguishes the present from the past and the future from the present. It therefore permits, if not dictates, a sense of progress: "A progressive, temporally oriented mythology arose, of a creation, once and for all, at the beginning of time, a subsequent fall, and a work of restoration, still in progress" (1962:7). On the one hand the physical world was created rather than is pre-existent. There is therefore a distinction between the time before its creation and the time since. On the other hand the physical world will one day be purified rather than dissolve. There is therefore a distinction between the time before its purification and the time after. As Campbell says of the Western outlook of Zoroastrianism:

> ... the Zoroastrian version of the world course presents a creation by a god of pure light into which an evil principle entered, by nature contrary to and independent of the first, so that there is a cosmic battle in progress; which, however, is not to go on forever, but will terminate in a total victory of the light: whereupon the process will end in a perfect realization of the Kingdom of Righteousness on Earth, and there will be no continuation of the cycle. There is no idea here of eternal return. (1962:244)

The East, says Campbell, makes no distinctions among past, present, and future. More precisely, it makes no distinction between the past and the future, for the future is only a return to the past. There is, then, a cycle rather than progress:

> The myth of eternal return, which is still basic to Oriental life, displays an order of fixed forms that appear and reappear through all time. The daily round of the sun, the waning and waxing moon, the cycle of the year, and the rhythm of organic birth, death, and new birth, represent a miracle of continuous arising that is fundamental to the nature of the universe. We all know the archaic myth of the four ages of gold, silver, bronze, and iron, where the world is shown declining, growing ever worse. It will disintegrate presently in chaos, only to burst forth again, fresh as a flower, to recommence spontaneously the inevitable course. There never was a time when time was not. Nor will there be a time when this kaleidoscopic play of eternity in time will have ceased. (1964:3)

Even if there is a distinction between the time before creation and the time since, and even if there is a distinction between the time since and the time of the envisioned end, there is none between the time before creation and the time of the

envisioned end. For the end envisioned is the dissolution of creation and the return
to the time before it.

DIFFERENCES IN THE CONCEPTS OF GOD AND MAN

West and East differ over not only temporal distinctions but also spatial and,
more, metaphysical ones. Campbell notes the spatial distinction drawn in the West
and denied in the East between god and the world: where in the West god is
transcendent, in the East god is immanent. Campbell emphasizes much more the
ontological distinction drawn in the West and denied in the East between god and
man: where in the West god is above man, in the East man is identical with god.
Where in the West man seeks to obey god, in the East he seeks to become god.
Where, as Campbell likes to put it, man in the West seeks a "relationship" with
god, in the East he seeks unity with god. More accurately, he seeks to realize the
unity he innately has:

> In the Indian version it is the god himself that divides and becomes
> not man alone but all creation; so that everything is a manifestation
> of that single inhabiting divine substance: there is no other; whereas
> in the Bible, God and man, from the beginning, are distinct. Man is
> made in the image of God, indeed, and the breath of God has been
> breathed into his nostrils; yet his being, his self, is not that of God,
> nor is it one with the universe.... God is transcendent.... The goal ...
> has to be, rather, to know the *relationship* of God to his creation,
> or more specifically, to man, and through such knowledge, by God's
> grace, to link one's own will back to that of the Creator. (1962:10-
> 11)

A further consequence of the separation in the West between man and god is
that kings are merely human. In the East they are divine. In the West kings may be
the representatives of gods and may therefore be higher than other humans, but
humans they remain. In the East, by contrast, kings are simply those humans who
have realized their divinity more fully than others. Campbell thus contrasts the
merely human status of later Sumerian kings--earlier ones being part of the Eastern
outlook--to the outright divine one of Egyptian ones, whom he considers Eastern:

> For the Mesopotamian [i.e., later Sumerian] kings were no longer, like
> those of Egypt, gods in themselves. That critical dissociation between
> the spheres of God and man which in time was to separate decisively
> the religious systems of the Occident from those of the Orient, had
> already taken place. The king was no longer a god-king ... but only the
> "vicar" ... of the true King, who was the god above. (1962:107)[2]

As a striking case of the belief in the divinity of kings Campbell cites (1962:4-
5) James Frazer's description of the ritualistic killing of kings to insure the

continuing health of the god of vegetation residing in them and therefore of vegetation itself.[3] But where Frazer considers this scheme universal, Campbell restricts it to the East, for it presupposes the belief in the divinity of the king. Where Campbell assumes that in the East all mankind is divine, Frazer restricts divinity worldwide to the king, who for that reason is alone killed.

This distinction between West and East does not seem exaggerated. The West indeed stresses the gap between man and god and is therefore basically nonmystical: its ideal is proximity to god, not union with him. The East indeed stresses the identity between man and god and so is fundamentally mystical: its ideal is outright oneness with god. Certainly there are Western mystics and Eastern nonmystics, but mysticism is still an overwhelmingly Eastern phenomenon. Most scholars, defining the term more broadly, argue that Western mystics do not even seek oneness with god but instead seek only the experience of god.[4] Some scholars allow for exceptions like the Gnostics and Meister Eckhart, but most argue that the preponderance of the greatest Western mystics--for example, St. Teresa of Avila and St. John of the Cross--seek less than outright oneness. And even scholars who argue that Western mystics, like their Eastern counterparts, seek outright oneness[5] grant that mysticism is a marginal activity in the West and a central one in the East.[6]

DIFFERENCES IN THE CONCEPT OF HEROISM

If, according to the East, man is divine, then, notes Campbell, all striving, which is to say all heroism, is vain: man already possesses whatever he might be seeking. In *Masks: Oriental*, as in *Masks: Occidental*, Campbell associates heroism with aggression and ambition rather than, as in *Hero*, with adventurousness and questing. Hence heroism in both *Masks: Oriental* and *Occidental* is a distinctively Western rather than universal phenomenon.

Where in *Masks: Occidental* Campbell roots heroism in patriarchy and its absence in matriarchy, in *Masks: Oriental* he attributes heroism to the belief in the separation between man and god and its absence to the belief in their identity. Striving makes no sense where man is already one with the object of his striving:

In the European West, ... where the fundamental doctrine of the freedom of the will essentially dissociates each individual from every other, as well as from both the will in nature and the will of God, there is placed upon each the responsibility of coming intelligently, out of his own experience and volition, to some sort of relationship with--not identity with or extinction in--the all, the void, the suchness, the absolute, or whatever the proper term may be for that which is beyond terms.... Not life as a good soldier, but life as a developed, unique individual, is the ideal. And we shall search the Orient in vain for anything quite comparable. There the ideal, on the contrary, is the quenching, not development, of ego. That is the formula turned this way and that, up and down the line, throughout the literature: a systematic, steady, continually drumming devaluation of the "I" principle .... (1962: 22-23)[7]

Campbell's most telling example of this difference between West and East is the contrast he draws between the individualistic striving of the Aryan invaders, who are Western, and the yearning by the conquered pre-Aryan inhabitants, who are Eastern, for absorption in the cosmos:

> Now, as we have seen, the mythological foundation of the Indus
> Civilization overthrown by the Aryans appears to have been a variant
> of the old High Bronze Age vegetal-lunar rhythmic order, wherein a
> priestly science of the calendar required of all submission without
> resistance to an ungainsayable destiny. The goddess mother in whose
> macrocosmic womb all things were supposed to live their brief lives
> was absolute in her sway; and no such puny sentiment as heroism
> could hope, in the field of her dominion, to achieve any serious result.
> "She is self-willed," said Ramakrishna, "and must always have her
> own way." Yet for those children who submit without tumult to their
> mother's will, "she is full of bliss." (1962:179)[8]

DIFFERENCES IN THE CONCEPTS OF REALITY

The West, for Campbell, preaches a division not only between man and god but also within man between his body and his soul. That division, or dualism, is a microcosm of the cosmic division between the physical world and a nonphysical one. By contrast, says Campbell, the East preaches the identity of not only man with god but also within man of his body with his soul. That identity, or monism, is in turn a microcosm of the identity of the physical with the nonphysical world.

Whether the undeniable difference between the beliefs of the West and those of the East is quite that between dualism and monism is debatable. Insofar as there is dualism in the West, that dualism takes either mild or radical form. Where the dualism is mild--for example, in the Gospels of Matthew and Mark, in most of Plato, and in Aristotle--the aim is merely to subordinate the body to the soul. The aim is to harmonize the parts of man under the control of the soul. Where the dualism is radical--for example, in the Gospel of John, in Paul, in Plato's *Phaedo*, and above all in Gnosticism--the aim is to reject the body for the soul. The aim is not to harmonize the parts of man but to disentangle them.

Where the West is not dualistic, mild or radical, it is monistic, ordinary or radical. Ordinary monism recognizes the existence of only the body. There is no soul. Much of the West is surely monistic--for example, Homer, Hesiod, and nearly all of the Old Testament. Values are worldly. The aim of life is prosperity, health, power, or even something intangible but still worldly like honor. There is no asceticism. There is no afterlife. Hades, for example, is really only a pale shadow of life before death. The body in this life is the sole reality. Where there is a yearning to escape from the body, it is because life is painful, not, as in radical dualism, because life is trivial or meaningless.[9]

Radical monism presupposes dualism, which it claims to transcend, just as dualism presupposes ordinary monism, which it claims to transcend. Just as dualism represents a stage beyond ordinary monism, so radical monism represents a stage beyond dualism.[10] Radical monism itself has two stages. Far more frequent in the West, in which radical monism of any kind is hardly plentiful, is radical monism of the tame kind. Here the soul alone is real, and the body is illusory--the reverse of ordinary monism. Valentinian Gnostics and Christian Scientists are examples. Both dismiss the body as not just inferior or even evil but unreal.

The radical variety of radical monism says that the single substance that exists is neither immateriality nor matter but rather a fusion of the two. Immateriality and matter, soul and body, prove to be one and the same. Western believers in this radical form of radical dualism include Meister Eckhart, William Blake, and Sir Arthur Eddington.

Dualism, radical or mild, may well, as Campbell says, be far more prevalent in the West than in the East, but ordinary monism may be even more prevalent. In any case radical monism is doubtless, as Campbell says, the prevailing belief in the East. The tame version is the more common. Virtually all of Buddhism and the dominant, Vedantic branch of Hinduism preach the freedom of the soul from the body, which is not, as in dualism, merely inferior or even evil but illusory. Tantrism and other branches of Hinduism espouse the radical variety of radical dualism. They thereby preach not the rejection of the body for the soul but the experience of the soul in the body--better, of the soul *as* the body.

MASKS AND HERO

In *Masks*, as noted, Campbell interprets Eastern myths the way in *Hero* he interprets all myths. On the one hand, contrary to *Hero*, Campbell in *Masks* limits heroism to the West. On the other hand, also contrary to *Hero*, he interprets heroism as striving for individual attainment rather than for absorption in the whole. In *Masks* Campbell says that only the East seeks unity and that heroism assumes individuality.

Yet Campbell's characterization of what in *Hero* he calls universal heroism is almost identical with what in *Masks* he calls distinctively Eastern nonheroism. In both cases the ideal is the radical form of radical monism: the experience of the oneness of the physical with the nonphysical world and of the body with the soul. As Campbell says of India, which for him, as for others, is the heart of the East:

> ... although the holy mystery and power have been understood to be indeed transcendent, ... they are also, at the same time, immanent ....
> It is not that the divine is every*where*: it is that the divine is every*thing*.
> So that one does not require any outside reference, revelation, sacrament, or authorized community to return to it. (1962: 12-13)[11]

In *Hero* all but the hero are ordinary monists: they are oblivious to even the possibility of a world beyond the everyday, physical one. They scorn the hero for believing otherwise. Before the call even he is oblivious. Were the hero's quest to end with his permanent separation from the everyday world, hero myths would be preaching either radical dualism or the tame variety of radical monism. If they preached that the everyday world is real but simply trivial or even evil, they would be preaching radical dualism. If they preached that the everyday world is outright illusory, they would be preaching radical monism of the tame variety.

For Campbell, hero myths preach instead return to the everyday world, but, as noted, it is far from clear why. At times Campbell says that the hero returns entirely selflessly to inform others of the existence of a higher reality, which they should in turn seek by forsaking the everyday one. In that case hero myths would still be espousing either radical dualism or the tame version of radical monism. More often, Campbell says that the hero, even in returning selflessly, discovers the existence of the higher reality within the everyday one. But "within" can still mean distinct from the everyday world, just intertwined with it or even trapped within it. In that case hero myths would clearly be preaching radical dualism. What, for Campbell, the hero in *Hero* really discovers is that the higher reality exists not within but *as* the everyday reality. He discovers that the two realities are one--the radical brand of radical monism that in *Masks* Campbell deems the distinctively Eastern view.[12]

AN ILLUSTRATION OF THE DIFFERENT CONCEPTS OF REALITY

A famous tale from one of the *Upanishads* best illustrates these different outlooks:

> "Explain more to me, father," said Svetaketu.
> "So be it, my son."
> "Place this salt in water and come to me tomorrow morning."
> Svetaketu did as he was commanded, and in the morning his father
>   said to him: "Bring me the salt you put into the water last night."
> Svetaketu looked into the water, but could not find it, for it had
>   dissolved.
> His father then said: "Taste the water from this side. How is it?"
> "It is salt."
> "Taste it from the middle. How is it?"
> "It is salt."
> "Taste it from that side. How is it?"
> "It is salt."
> "Look for the salt again and come again to me."
> The son did so, saying: "I cannot see the salt. I only see water."
> His father then said: "In the same way, O my son, you cannot see the
>   Spirit. But in truth he is here."[13]

An ordinary monist would, strictly, not even taste the salt, which corresponds to immateriality, and would experience only the water, which corresponds to matter. Better, he would not distinguish between the salt and the water. He would consider it all mere water, which simply happened to be salty.

A dualist would distinguish between the salt and the water. He would consider the salt an addition to the water. A mild dualist would merely care more about the salt than about the water. A radical dualist would seek to extricate the salt from the water, which he would then discard.

A radical monist of the tame sort would deny the reality of the water. He would claim that all was salt--the water being an illusion. An extreme radical monist would claim that the two substances were really one: that salt and water were really a single, salt-watery substance, not a mixture of once-distinct salt and water.

Svetaketu is preaching this extreme brand of radical monism to his son, who till now has likely been a dualist. Admittedly, the metaphor of salt and water is less than perfect: after all, salt can be added to water and perhaps even extracted from it, and both salt and water are physical substances. Still, the point is clear: just as salt ordinarily seems inextricable from water, so immateriality is inextricable from matter, in which case they constitute a single substance.

Only in passing in *Masks: Oriental* does Campbell associate Western mythology with patriarchy and Eastern with matriarchy. Indeed, only by implication does he associate the West with patriarchy, and he links the East less to a matriarchal society than to the supremacy of the mother goddess. As quoted (1962:179), he contrasts the independence of the mother sought by the West to the absorption in her sought by the East.[14] In *Masks: Oriental*, as in *Masks: Occidental*, Campbell occasionally ties the East to planting[15] but even less frequently, if at all, the West to hunting.

Campbell "psychologizes" myth far less in any of the volumes of *Masks* than in *Hero*. In *Masks* he uses psychology more as a metaphorical description of myth than as an actual explanation or interpretation of it. Still, he does say in *Masks: Oriental*, as in *Masks: Occidental* (1964:173-174), that the Western goal corresponds to the development of the ego and the Eastern one to its dissolution: "... spiritual maturity, as understood in the modern Occident, requires a differentiation of *ego* from *id*, whereas in the Orient ... ego ... is impugned as the principle of libidinous delusion, to be dissolved" (1962:15).[16] Where in *Masks* the dissolution of the ego is a distinctively Eastern goal, in *Hero* it is the universal one, though, as noted, Campbell wrongly interprets the hero's pseudo-return to the everyday world as the preservation of the ego.

NOTES

[1] On this difference between West and East see also Campbell, "On Mythic Shapes of Things to Come--Circular and Linear," *Horizon*, 16 (Summer 1974), 35-36.

2 See also Campbell 1962:6-7, 80, 101-102, 131-132, 167-168.

3 James G. Frazer, *The Golden Bough*, one-vol. abridgment (London: Macmillan, 1922), chs. 24-26.

4 See, for example, R. C. Zaehner, *Mysticism: Sacred and Profane* (New York: Oxford University, 1961), chs. 8-9; Gershom Scholem, *Major Trends in Jewish Mysticism* (New York: Schocken, 1954), ch. 1; Steven Katz, "Language, Epistemology, and Mysticism," in *Mysticism and Philosophical Analysis*, ed. Katz (New York: Oxford University, 1978), 26-74.

5 See, for example, Walter T. Stace, *Mysticism and Philosophy* (London: Macmillan 1961), ch. 2; Stace, *The Teachings of the Mystics* (New York: Mentor, 1960), 23-24, 126-130, 238.

6 See Stace, *The Teachings of the Mystics*, 124.

7 See also Campbell 1962:242-243.

8 See also Campbell 1962:181-189, 3-4. Campbell associates the East with not only an immanent deity but also an impersonal force. Conversely, he associates the West with not only a transcendent god but also a personal one. Since he stresses the irrevocable cyclicality of life for the East, it is not coincidental that he associates this impersonal force with fate. For example, citing a Sumerian flood story in which the flood is the result of the anger of a god, he contrasts that view, which for him represents a Semitic and therefore Western interpolation, to the fundamentally Sumerian and therefore Eastern view of the flood as the natural work of fate: see Campbell 1962:127. See also Campbell 1962:128-130, 180-189, 231-232, 243.

9 See Campbell 1962:137-140.

10 For differing sets of stages see, for example, Scholem, ch. 1; Robert N. Bellah, "Religious Evolution," *American Sociological Review*, 29 (June 1964), 358-374.

11 To be sure, since Campbell says that the East espouses radical monism of the tame as well as the strong form, to the West's striving in the physical world he sometimes contrasts the East's utter rejection of that world rather than identification of it with the nonphysical world: see Campbell 1962: 232-233, 244-245.

12 Following others, Stace (*Mysticism and Philosophy*, 61-111, 131-133; *The Teachings of the Mystics*, 14-23) distinguishes between what he calls "extrovertive" and what he calls "introvertive" mysticism. Extrovertive mysticism finds ultimate reality within the physical world. It uses the senses to discover that reality. Introvertive mysticism finds ultimate reality outside the physical world. It uses the mind rather than the senses to discover that reality. Extrovertive mysticism

usually corresponds to radical monism of the extreme variety. Though Stace deems introvertive mysticism higher, it corresponds to something less extreme: either radical dualism or radical monism of the tame variety. But since, for Stace, both brands of mysticism preach the oneness of all things, there can be no radical dualism, in which case introvertive mysticism must be preaching radical monism rather than radical dualism. Though Stace himself does not consider the possibility, there are extrovertive mystics who are radical monists of the tame variety--for example, Emerson, Thoreau, and Lao-Tse. They find ultimate reality *in* the physical world yet paradoxically deem only the nonphysical world real. Ordinarily, however, extrovertive mysticism deems the physical world real, just simultaneously more than physical.

[13] Chandogya Upanishad, in *The Upanishads*, tr. Juan Mascaro (Harmondsworth, Middlesex, England: Penguin, 1965), 117-118.

[14] See also Campbell 1962:164-168.

[15] See *ibid.*

[16] See also Campbell 1962:22.

Chapter Six

THE MASKS OF GOD: CREATIVE MYTHOLOGY

In one prime respect *Masks: Creative Mythology* constitutes a break with the rest of *Masks* and a return to *Hero*: in its endorsement of heroism. Though Campbell does not discuss heroism in the first volume of *Masks*, in volumes two and three he denigrates it as the epitome of the divisive, self-centered, futile striving of the individualistic West. In contrast to it stands the passive absorption in the whole wisely sought by the East. In volumes two and three of *Masks* the hero strives to conquer the world, not to help others. His striving assumes a gap not only between him and others but also between him and god. It is this gap which he is seeking to overcome. He is ultimately seeking to become god himself. Because the East assumes the identity of not only all humans with one another but also humans with god, it denies the gulf that heroism yearns to overcome.

In *Hero*, by contrast, heroism is a universal, not merely Western, enterprise. Moreover, it presupposes the very beliefs that in volumes two and three of *Masks* make it Eastern and therefore nonheroic. In *Hero* the hero is still striving, but for oneness with the cosmos, not for control over it. Indeed, he is seeking to realize the oneness he innately has. He is seeking not to become god but to realize his divinity. He is, moreover, acting on behalf of others, not or not just himself. He is still heroic, for he must still undertake a daring journey to an unknown land, but his heroism is peaceful rather than hostile.

In several ways volume four of *Masks* represents a return to *Hero*. First, heroism again is universal rather than particularly Western. Second, heroism is mystical: the hero seeks to realize his oneness with the cosmos rather than to gain control over it. Third, heroism is selfless rather than self-centered: the hero seeks to share his discovery with others. Fourth, heroism requires the same dangerous trek to a strange world and return from it.

Masks: Creative is not, however, a sheer return to *Hero*. Heroism now is "creative." The new, creative hero is not, however, the subject of hero myths, who remains the same, but his creator.

Following others, Campbell characterizes the period of creative mythology, the middle of the twelfth century on, as one of a loss of faith, at least faith in orthodox, institutionalized Christianity. The modern loss of faith conventionally ascribed to the rise of science Campbell considers a continuation of this earlier one. The consequence of the loss of faith in the late medieval period was the loss of traditional myths, which for Campbell had always been tied to religion. Where, according to Campbell, previous mankind, primitive and Eastern as well as Western, had existing myths to guide it, Western man since 1150 or so has had to invent his own:

> In the context of a traditional mythology, the symbols are presented
> in socially maintained rites, through which the individual is required
> to experience ... certain insights, sentiments, and commitments. In
> what I am calling "creative" mythology, on the other hand, this order
> is reversed: the individual has had an experience of his own--of order,
> horror, beauty, or even mere exhilaration--which he seeks to
> communicate through signs; and if his realization has been of a
> certain depth and import, his communication will have the value and
> force of living myth--for those, that is to say, who receive and
> respond to it of themselves, with recognition, uncoerced. (1968: 4)[1]

It is, then, the mythmakers themselves who are Campbell's distinctively modern heroes. Chief among them are Gottfried von Strassburg, author of *Tristan*; Wolfram von Eschenbach, author of *Parzival*; James Joyce; and Thomas Mann. As Campbell declares elsewhere, "Perhaps the artist is the best prototype of the modern hero. James Joyce or Thomas Mann, for instance, have [sic] created a new mythology."[2]

Because Campbell considers only the later medieval and modern West to be bereft of traditional myths, he considers only it to be capable of creative mythology. Repeatedly, he contrasts the originality and individuality of the later West to the rigidity and conformity of not just the earlier West but the East and primitive peoples:

> And so we may say in summary at this point that the first and
> absolutely essential characteristic of the new ... mythology that was
> emerging in the literature of the twelfth and thirteenth centuries
> was that its structuring themes were not derived from dogma,
> learning, politics, or any current concepts of the general social good,
> but were expressions of individual experience: what I have termed
> Libido as opposed to Credo.... Traditional mythologies, that is to say,
> whether of the primitive or of the higher cultures, antecede and
> control experience; whereas what I am here calling Creative
> Mythology is an effect and expression of experience. (1968:64-65)

Campbell goes much farther in praise of creative mythology. He credits it with not just a new set of heroes but a new definition of heroism. Despite his praising both universal heroism in *Hero* and the nonheroism of the East in *Masks: Occidental* and *Oriental* for exactly their affirmation rather than rejection of the everyday, physical world, Campbell now singles out creative mythology as alone affirming the physical world, which, he now says, all past mythology rejects. The epitome of this affirmation is, for him, courtly love, as represented by not only *Tristan* but also *Parzival.*

GOTTFRIED'S *TRISTAN*

At the outset of his analysis of *Tristan*[3] Campbell expresses amazement that anyone could interpret the work as Gnostic, which is to say as radically dualistic rather than monistic:

> I find it impossible to understand how anyone who had really read
> both the literature of Gnosticism and the poetry of Gottfried could
> suggest--as does a recent student of the psychology of *amor*--that
> not only Gottfried but also the other Tristan poets, and the
> troubadors as well, were Manichaeans. (1968:175)

Tristan, assumes Campbell, accepts the physical world rather than, like the Gnostics, rejects it:

> ... whereas according to the Gnostic-Manichaean view nature is
> corrupt and the lure of the senses to be repudiated, in the poetry of
> the troubadors, in the Tristan story, and in Gottfried's work above all,
> nature in its noblest moment--the realization of love--is an end and
> glory in itself; and the senses, ennobled and refined by courtesy and
> art, temperance, loyalty and courage, are the guides to this
> realization. (1968:176)

Invoking a distinction that he applies more fully to the Grail legend, Campbell asserts that the Tristan story defines the ideal form of love as neither *eros*, which, as lust, amounts to sheer worldliness and so to ordinary monism, nor *agape*, which, as selfless, brotherly love, is equivalent to otherworldliness and so to radical dualism, but *amor*, which somehow combines the two to constitute the radical variety of radical monism:

> It is amazing, but our theologians still are writing of *agape* and *eros*
> and their radical opposition, as though these two were the final terms
> of the principle of "love": the former, "charity," godly and spiritual,
> being "of men toward each other in a community," and the latter,
> "lust," natural and fleshly, being "the urge, desire and delight of sex."
> Nobody in a pulpit seems ever to have heard of *amor* as a third,
> selective, discriminating principle in contrast to the other two.
> (1968:177)[4]

Tristan, for Campbell, espouses radical monism in its radical form because it fuses heaven with earth, which in man means the soul with the body. For it finds the soul in the body rather than beyond it. One need not transcend the body to find the soul:

> For there is no such thing as a love that is either purely spiritual or merely sensual. Man is composed of body and spirit (if we may still use such terms) and is thus an essential mystery in himself; and the deepest heart of this mystery (in Gottfried's view) is the very point touched and wakened by--and in--the mystery of love, the sacramental purity of which has nothing whatsoever to do with a suspension or suppression of the sensuous and the senses, but includes and even rests upon the physical realization. (1968:248)

Campbell does not deny that the love of Tristan and Isolde leads to their deaths. Death, he laments, is simply the price of love. What he denies is the radically dualistic view of Richard Wagner and others that the couple's love culminates after death in a necessarily otherworldly, nonphysical form--a form that, despite his past characterization of the East as world affirming, he now labels "Oriental":

> And so there came to pass that death of both, of which Brangaene had foretold: Tristan of love, Isolt of pity. She stretched her body to his, laid her mouth to his, yielded her spirit, and expired. Which is the death that Wagner rendered as the love-death--with an Oriental turn, however, borrowed from Schopenhauer, of the transcendence of duality in extinction. (1968:255)

Most scholars agree with Campbell that the love of Tristan and Isolde ceases with their deaths. Whatever fulfillment they secure must be secured on earth, which is what makes their continuing separation so poignant. But the same scholars do not, like Campbell, therefore conclude happily that love and life coincide. They do not, like Campbell, conclude that *Tristan* thereby espouses the radical form of radical monism rather than radical dualism.

For if, as Campbell himself grants, love leads to death, then love and life, which means life in this world, are incompatible. The love of Blancheflor for Rivalin does heal him, but she nearly dies when Rivalin tells her that he is going off to war, and she does die in a premature childbirth indirectly induced by her grieving over his death in battle. Tristan, the son conceived during Blancheflor's healing of Rivalin, is thus the product of both love and death.

The potion that Isolde's mother brews for her daughter and King Mark at once intensifies, if not outright causes, the love of Tristan and Isolde and certainly causes their deaths. Indeed, they would have died at the outset from their separation if Isolde's servant Brangane had not consented to their union. Once united, they cannot bear further separation, which constitutes a living death. The literal death of one causes the same in the other: Tristan dies of a broken heart upon being falsely informed that Isolde has not come to heal him, and Isolde dies upon discovering his body.

The opposition between life in the cave and life in society underscores the opposition between love and life. Tristan and Isolde must flee society for the cave, located deep in the forest, in order to consummate their love. To say that society opposes only adultery, not physical love itself, is to miss the point: that courtly love, which Campbell deems the finest expression of worldly love, is inherently adulterous. To note that the pair return voluntarily to society is to miss the point as well: that they return only out of duty, which remains at odds with their love. Indeed, Tristan must eventually flee Mark's court altogether.

Undeniably, Tristan and Isolde attain spiritual bliss *through* physical intercourse. But sex is only the means, not the end, which is wholly spiritual. Indeed, the pair seek to transcend their bodies, which stand in the way of their final goal: not just reaching but unifying their souls. Life in the body thus precludes the attainment of this goal even in the cave. In short, *Tristan* lies closer to radical dualism than, as Campbell takes it, to the radical variety of radical monism.

WOLFRAM'S *PARZIVAL*

Campbell argues that Wolfram's version of the Grail legend,[5] like Gottfried's *Tristan*, espouses the same kind of radical monism: the soul lies within the body, ultimate reality within everyday reality. Better put: the soul *is* the body; ultimate reality *is* everyday reality. Campbell thus contrasts Wolfram's version, in which the hero is Parzival, to the radically dualistic one of the Cistercian Fathers' *La Queste del Saint Graal*,[6] in which the hero is Galahad:

> The Grail here [i.e., in Wolfram], as in the later *Queste*, is the symbol of supreme spiritual value. It is attained, however, not by renouncing the world or even current social custom, but, on the contrary, by participation with every ounce of one's force in the century's order of life in the way or ways dictated by one's own uncorrupted heart ....
> (1968:564)

Undeniably, Parzival is a far more worldly knight than Galahad. Where Galahad is free of worldly values from the start, Parzival must be weaned away from them. Where Galahad immediately recognizes the otherworldly meaning of the Grail, Parzival grasps it only slowly. Where Galahad, upon partaking of the Mass with the Grail, ascends to heaven, Parzival remains on earth as the successor to the Fisher King.

Where above all Galahad is celibate, Parzival is married. For Campbell, Parzival's ability to secure the Grail without forsaking his wife epitomizes the ideal blend of otherworldliness and worldliness that constitutes radical monism, which henceforth will mean in its radical form. Indeed, Campbell characterizes Parzival's relationship to Condwiramurs, his wife, as one of *amor* rather than either *eros*, which Gawain embodies, or *agape*, which not only Galahad but also the later Parzival of both Wagner and Alfred Lord Tennyson represents:

Condwiramurs, like Parzival, stood for a new ideal, a new possibility
in love and life: namely, of love (*amor*) as the sole motive for
marriage and an indissoluble marriage as the sacrament of love--
whereas in the normal manner of that period the sacrament was held
as far as possible apart from the influence of *amor*, to be governed
by the concerns only of security and reputation, politics and
economics: while love, known only as *eros*, was to be sublimated as
agape, and if any such physical contact occurred as would not become
either a monk or a nun, it was to be undertaken dutifully, as far as
possible without pleasure, for God's purpose of repopulating those
vacant seats in Heaven which had been emptied when the wicked
angels fell. (1968:456)

The duty that Parzival rejects thus involves not only abstinence but also social
convention: Parzival rejects the daughter of the knight Gurnemanz as his wife
because he does not love her.

Campbell views the Parzival story as the legacy of a pre-Christian, Celtic,
radically monistic tradition. The Galahad story represents a later "Christianizing" of
the Parzival version by radically dualistic monks.[7]

At the same time Campbell considers Wolfram the *creator* of a secular
mythology, if somehow still a Christian one:

Moreover, he [Wolfram] applied his interpretations consciously to an
altogether *secular* mythology, of men and women living for *this*
world, not "that," pursuing earthly, human, and humane (i.e., in
Wolfram's terms, "courtly") purposes, and supported in their spiritual
tasks not by a supernatural grace dispensed by way of sacraments but
by the *natural* grace of individual endowment and the worldly virtue
of loyalty in love. That is what gives to his work its epochal
significance as the first example in the history of world literature of
a *consciously developed secular Christian myth*. (1968:476)

In the name of radical monism, whether or not of the Celtic outlook, Campbell
does, however, go too far. The Parzival version is incontestably more worldly than
the Galahad one, but it is at least as dualistic as monistic. To begin with, Parzival
must outright reject many worldly values, not simply fuse them with otherworldly
ones. Most conspicuously, he loses the Grail the first time because, as Campbell
himself stresses, he abides by knightly etiquette in refusing to query the Fisher
King:

The Round Table stands in Wolfram's work for the social order of the
period of which it was the summit and consummation. The young
knight's concern for his reputation as one worthy of that circle was
his motive for holding his tongue when his own better nature was
actually pressing him to speak; and in the light of his conscious
notion of himself as a knight worthy of the name, just hailed as the

greatest in the world, one can understand his shock and resentment at the sharp judgments of the Loathly Damsel and Sigune. However, those two were the messengers of a deeper sphere of values and possibilities than was yet known, or even sensed, by his socially conscious mind; they were of the sphere not of the Round Table but of the Castle of the Grail, which had not been a feature of the normal daylight world, visible to all, but dreamlike, visionary, mythic .... It had appeared to him as the first sign and challenge of a kingdom yet to be earned, beyond the sphere of the world's flattery, proper to his own unfolding life .... (1968:454)

Even if Parzival eventually returns to his wife, it is hardly clear how physical their relationship is. As Campbell himself notes (1968:440-443), the pair establish a spiritual bond, one involving abstinence, before they establish a physical one, which at the least therefore seems less important. Before meeting his wife, Parzival, in preparation for finding the Grail, must resist the temptation of sex with the wife of the knight Orilus. The objection here is seemingly to more than the fact of adultery. For Campbell himself judges the adulterous liaison of Tristan and Isolde *amor* rather than *eros*.

Parzival may return to rule over the Grail Kingdom rather than, like Galahad, ascend to heaven, but the Kingdom itself is otherworldly. Indeed, it is visible only to those who are ready for it.

Finally, Galahad, not Parzival, has always been the most popular hero of the Grail saga. It would therefore be hard to deem Parzival the representative Grail hero. Even if one judged the Parzival account radically monistic rather than dualistic, the Grail saga generally, as represented by Galahad, would therefore remain dualistic.

Because Wolfram considers the Grail itself a precious stone rather than, as in other versions, a cup, he is often assumed to be an alchemist. The stone would be the philosopher's stone, used to catalyze the transformation of base metals into gold or silver. In that case Wolfram would indeed be a radical monist: because immateriality, for alchemists, lies latent in matter, the two substances are really one. Parzival would be discovering that the Grail Kingdom lies *in* the everyday, material world, not outside it. As Campbell puts it alchemically, "The stone ... will bring us ... back to the world--as gold" (1968:430).

But in likely associating Wolfram with alchemy, Campbell ignores the far more common association of him with Catharism. As a form of medieval Gnosticism, Catharism was uncompromisingly dualistic.[8] If Wolfram were a Cathar, he would be espousing the utter rejection of the material world for the immaterial godhead. He would hardly be preaching return to the material world.

Indeed, Jessie Weston, whom Campbell cites approvingly[9] for precisely her interpretation of the Grail story as originally pre-Christian and then heterodox Christian, views the saga as the continuation of an ancient, esoteric, otherworldly tradition, only the public, exoteric side of which--the sole side recognized by Frazer--was worldly:

The Grail story is not *du fond en comble* the product of imagination, literary or popular. At its root lies the record ... of an ancient Ritual, having for its ultimate object the initiation into the secret of the sources of Life, physical and spiritual. This ritual, in its lower, exoteric form, as affecting the processes of Nature, and physical life, survives to-day .... In its esoteric "Mystery" form it was freely utilized for the imparting of high spiritual teaching concerning the relation of Man to the Divine Source of his being, and the possibility of a sensible union between Man, and God.[10]

Admittedly, Weston herself interprets the esoteric side of the Grail cult as merely far higher than the exoteric one rather than opposed to it, but so much higher is the esoteric side that the difference amounts to near-rejection of the exoteric, material side and so is almost identical with radical dualism. In fact, Weston deems the ancient practitioners of the esoteric side Gnostics.[11] To be sure, she does not say that these esoteric practitioners judged matter outright evil. Rather, they judged it merely inferior, but, again, so hopelessly inferior as nearly to reject it altogether.

To the extent that Campbell relies on Weston's interpretation the Grail story is, then, preaching something far more akin to radical dualism than to radical monism. When he praises her for showing "that the aim of the Grail Quest was originally [i.e., as pre-Christian] the restoration to life, health, and fecundity of a land, its people, and its king,"[12] he is reversing her main point.

Oddly, in a long essay elsewhere on the Grail legend[13] Campbell, without mentioning Weston, actually connects Wolfram to the Cathars, or Albigensians--a connection he never draws in *Masks*.[14] Yet he somehow then characterizes the Albigensians as radical monists rather than dualists.

Indeed, in *Masks: Creative* itself Campbell alternatively characterizes medieval Gnosticism as monistic and dualistic. On the one hand he says, as cited, that the world-rejecting dualism of Gnosticism makes it even farther afield of the radical monism of *Tristan* than the milder, if still radical, dualism of orthodox Christianity (1968:175-176, 230). On the other hand he links courtly love, and so presumably both *Tristan* and *Parzival*, to Gnosticism (1968:162-171), which he then links to the radical monism of the East (1968:149-161):

Hence, although the usual Gnostic attitude was strictly dualistic, striving ... to separate spirit from matter, with a strong sense of repugnance for the world, it is also possible to find in certain other Gnostic remains passages of inspiring affirmation; as, for instance, the words attributed to Jesus in the Gnostic Gospel "According to Thomas": "The Kingdom of the Father is spread upon the earth and men do not see it"; or again: "The Kingdom is within you and is without you. If you will know yourselves, then you will be known and you will know that you are the sons of the Living Father."... And, as we have learned from numerous Mahayana Buddhist texts of exactly the period of these Gnostic Perates, there is a "Wisdom of the Yonder Shore," ... which is, in fact, the ultimate wisdom of Buddhist realization; namely, a knowledge beyond all such dualistic conceptions as matter and spirit, bondage and release, sorrow and bliss. (1968:157)[15]

Campbell assumes that because divinity, or immateriality, lies within the material world, immateriality and matter are one, in which case there is radical monism. But in fact immateriality lies trapped in matter, from which it is irremediably distinct. The two substances are not like salt and water in the tale from the *Upanishads.* Christ is to be found not in the bodies but in the souls of his followers. Their souls may exist within their bodies, but, again, trapped in them and so distinct from them. Not coincidentally, the Gospel of Thomas preaches rejection of the body, sexually and otherwise; rejection of the material world; rejection of the Old Testament for exactly its approval of this world; salvation as the return of the immaterial souls to the immaterial godhead, from which they originally fell; and docetism, the doctrine that Jesus, the Gnostic savior, only seemingly had a body. When Campbell describes another Gnostic group as believing that "since Christ, the Son of the Father, is entrapped in the field of Matter, the whole universe is the cross on which the Son is crucified" (1968:161), he is clearly confusing entrapment with identity. Only by so doing can he claim that even if orthodox Christianity of the Middle Ages was radically dualistic, a sophisticated elite, one including both Gottfried and Wolfram, was radically monistic.

MANN AND JOYCE

Campbell regards Thomas Mann[16] and James Joyce[17] as the twentieth-century counterparts to Gottfried and Wolfram. He sees the heroes of "Tonio Kroger," *Buddenbrooks, The Magic Mountain, Joseph and His Brothers, A Portrait of the Artist as a Young Man, Ulysses,* and *Finnegans Wake* as persons daring enough not only to venture forth to a strange new world but also to return. Art rather than love is their entrée to that world. These heroes are not selfless. They return to the everyday world not because they want to spread the word to others but because they discover the new world within the everyday one. Unlike radical dualists, they need not forsake the body for the soul, earth for heaven, or man for god. As radical monists, they find the soul in the body, heaven on earth, and god in man. More precisely, they find that the soul is the body, that heaven is earth, and that god is man. What Campbell says of the difference between Joyce's outlook and the orthodox Roman Catholic one applies equally, for Campbell, to the difference between Mann's outlook and the mainstream Protestant one:

But between Joyce's and the Roman Catholic clergy's ways of interpreting Christian symbols there is a world of difference. The artist reads them in the universally known old Greco-Roman, Celto-Germanic, Hindu-Buddhist-Taoist, Neoplatonic way, as referring to an experience of the mystery beyond theology that is immanent in all things, including gods, demons, and flies. The priests, on the other

hand, are insisting on the absolute finality of their Old Testament
concept of a personal creator God "out there," who, though
omnipresent, omniscient, and omni-everything-else, is ontologically
distinct from the living substance of his world .... (1968:260-261)

Specifically, Campbell contrasts the outlook of Hans Castorp, the hero of
Mann's *Magic Mountain*, to that of his two would-be mentors: the optimistic,
liberal, progressive, humanist Settembrini, and the pessimistic, cynical, Marxist,
Jesuit Naphta. Where Settembrini preaches a worldly human improvement that
corresponds to ordinary monism, Naphta espouses a world-rejecting religiosity that
amounts to radical dualism:

> One [i.e., Settembrini] is defending the glory of man and the spirit as
> revealed in the faculty of reason; the other [i.e., Naphta], God and the
> spirit transcendent, absolutely apart from and against fallen, natural
> man, his instincts, reason, pretensions to freedom, progress, science,
> rights, and all the rest. Naphta charges Settembrini with the heresy
> of [ordinary] monism; Settembrini, Naphta with [radical] dualism and
> world-splitting. (1968:380)

Hans does indeed learn from both, but he learns above all to reject the extremes
they embody. He learns on the one hand that there exists more than the everyday
world of ordinary monism--the world below that he has left behind for the
sanitorium--but on the other hand that he, like Campbell's hero in *Hero*, need not
reject the everyday world for the deeper, higher one. For the two are really one.
Hence Hans finally leaves the sanitorium for the world below:

> The young engineer [i.e., Hans] was able to recognize ... in the
> arguments of Naphta ... a depth of insight into the woes of the world
> that went beyond that of his other mentor, Settembrini. However, the
> separation by Naphta of the values of the spirit from those of living
> in this world with love for it as it is, left him unconvinced. Pain,
> sickness, death and corruption, indeed: but were these a refutation of
> life? (1968:382)[18]

On the one hand Campbell says that Joyce has the same world-affirming
outlook as Mann.[19] On the other hand he sometimes says that Joyce rejects the
world:

> Thus the abyss that Hans refused, and together with Hans his author,
> Joyce and his characters entered .... [W]e are presented [in Mann and
> Joyce] with opposed experiences and representations of the
> archetypes of our lives: that of the soul of light, so to say, and that of
> the soul of darkness; in the language of the Bible: Abel and Cain, Isaac
> and Ishmael, Jacob and Esau, Joseph and his brothers. Mann identified
> with Jacob and Joseph, Joyce with Esau and Cain; i.e., Mann with the

one who wins in the light world, Joyce with the one who loses
there .... (1968:661)

Despite Campbell's singling out Joyce, even more than Mann, as his chief
contemporary hero and so surely as a radical monist, he never reconciles his
monistic reading with this dualistic one.

INDIVIDUALISM

In volumes two and three of *Masks* the East is Campbell's ideal. Suddenly, in
volume four, together with several essays in *The Flight of the Wild Gander* and
Myths to Live By,[20] the West, from the twelfth century on, is his ideal, and the
East becomes his nemesis. Where, in volumes two and three of *Masks*, Campbell
praises the East for its nonheroic yearning for the absorption of the individual in the
cosmic whole, now in *Masks: Creative* he condemns what he labels the East's
oppressive, even totalitarian subordination of the individual to the whole, which is
here social as well as cosmic. Where, in volumes two and three of *Masks*,
Campbell scorns the West for its stress on the petty, selfish, and vain striving of the
individual,[21] now in *Masks: Creative* he upholds individuality as indispensably
human. What Campbell says elsewhere makes it clear that he is endorsing, not
merely describing, this romantic individualism:

It is my thought, that the wealth and glory of the Western world, and
of the modern world as well (in so far as it is still in spirit Western),
is a function of this respect for the individual, not as a member of
some sanctified consensus through which he is given worth, ... nor as
an indifferent name and form of that "same perfection and infinity ...
present in every grain of sand, and in the raindrop as much as in the
sea," ... but as an end and value in himself, unique in his *im*perfection,
i.e., in his yearning, in his process of becoming not what he "ought" to
be but what he is, actually and potentially: such a one as was never
seen before. (1969:222-223)

It is above all Wolfram's *Parzival* that marks the new age. That age at last frees
man from, first, submission to god:

In Wolfram's *Parzival* the boon is to be the inauguration of a new age
of the human spirit: of *secular* spirituality, sustained by self-
responsible individuals acting not in terms of general laws supposed
to represent the will or way of some personal god or impersonal
eternity, but each in terms of his own developing realization of worth.
Such an idea is distinctly--and uniquely--European. (1968:480)

The new age frees man from, second, submission to the group:

The Indian notion of *sva–dharma*, "one's own duty," [seemingly] suggests comparison: "Better is one's own dharma, imperfectly performed, than the dharma of another, performed to perfection," states the *Bhagavad Gītā*. However, the idea of duty there is of the duties of one's caste, as defined by the timeless ... Indian social order. The Westerner reading such a text might think of duties self-imposed, self-discovered, self-assumed: a vocation elected and realized. That is not the Oriental idea. Nor is the Oriental "person" the same as ours.... The "indwelling being" is the reincarnating monad; and the aim of a well-lived lifetime is not to realize the unique possibilities of its temporal embodiment, but on the contrary, to achieve such indifference to this body and its limitations, potentialities, and vicissitudes, that, "completely devoid of the sense of 'I' and 'mine,' one attains peace." (1968:480-481)[22]

Campbell contrasts "creative" mythology to that of not only the East but also primitives and the earlier West. As he says of the individualistic tenets of creative mythology, "In the long course of our survey of the mythologies of mankind we have encountered nothing quite like this" (1968:480). Still, he regards the East as the culture most fervently opposed to individualism, though in at least a few places[23] he castigates the earlier West--Judaism, Christianity, and Islam--even more severely than it.

What accounts for the reversal of Campbell's views? Campbell himself never says, though an interviewer attributes it to Campbell's revulsion toward the India he had long revered but not visited until 1954:

In 1954, after thirty years of being so immersed in Eastern art, philosophy, and religion that he considered himself "almost a Hindu," Campbell traveled to India. And the gods played apple-basket-turnover. He was so appalled by the caste system and the lack of respect for the individual that he returned a confirmed Westerner, celebrating the uniqueness of the person.[24]

Two critics of Campbell's[25] likewise struck by the abrupt shift in his assessment of East and West attribute it to the Cold War. According to them, *Hero*, written at the end of World War II, evinces the postwar American belief in world peace and unity. *Masks*, written in the Fifties and Sixties, expresses the subsequent American opposition to the totalitarianism of not only Russia but also the Third World.

It is true that Campbell voices his pro-Western, anti-Eastern convictions as early as the 1957 essay "The Symbol without Meaning."[26] But these commentators fail to account for his praise of the East in volumes two and three of *Masks*, which were published as late as 1962 and 1964. Conversely, they cannot account for his hostility to the East as late as 1968, when not only volume four of *Masks* but also the essay "The Secularization of the Sacred"[27] appeared. Surely by then the Cold War had begun to ebb.[28]

In volumes one and three of *Masks* Campbell thematically parallels, if not quite equates, the mythology of primitive planters with that of the East and the mythology of primitive hunters with that of the West. At the outset of *Masks: Occidental* (1964:5-6)[29] Campbell goes so far as to characterize the Eastern outlook as the continuation of that of primitive planters, though not quite the Western one as the continuation of that of primitive hunters.

In his essay "The Symbol without Meaning" (Campbell 1969:ch. 5), which is otherwise largely a sketch of *Masks: Primitive*, Campbell proceeds to parallel, if likewise not quite equate, the mythology of primitive hunters with that of not the West per se but only the West from the twelfth century on: the West of individualistic striving free from the tyranny of either god or society. Where in *Masks: Creative* the individualism espoused by creative mythology is unprecedented, in "The Symbol without Meaning" it is a restoration of that of primitive hunters, who in at least *Masks: Primitive* have the oldest brand of mythology.[30] The forerunners of later Westerners, primitive hunters are here self-sufficient and rigidly independent:

> ... today, when the mandala itself, the whole structure of meaning to which society and its guardians would attach us, is dissolving, what is required of us all, spiritually as well as corporeally, is much more the fearless self-sufficiency of our shamanistic inheritance [i.e., hunters] than the timorous piety of the priest-guided Neolithic [i.e., planters].... The creative researches and wonderful daring of our scientists today partake far more of the lion spirit of shamanism than of the piety of priest and peasant. (1969:189, 192)[31]

Where, in volumes one and three of *Masks*, Campbell proceeds to dismiss the very differences between hunters and planters and between West and East that he so labors to explicate, now, in volume four, he retains them. Where, in volumes one and three, Campbell not only denigrates but finally denies the would-be distinctive outlook of hunters and Westerners--consciously or unconsciously, hunters are really planters and Westerners Easterners--now he maintains that hunters and later Westerners have a distinctive, not to say superior, outlook. Primitive hunters and later Westerners are really, not just apparently, the opposite of primitive planters, earlier Westerners, and the East for all time.

In other works Campbell virtually identifies mythology with religion.[32] In *Masks: Creative* he severs the two: creative mythology is secular rather than religious, though, consistently or not, Campbell characterizes not only Mann and Joyce as religious but Wolfram's *Parzival*, his prime example, as a "secular Christian myth" (1968:476).

In other works Campbell does not, it is true, stress the third, social function of myth--socialization--but as one of the four functions of myth he certainly approves of it.[33] In *Masks: Creative* he scorns it as the subordination of the individual to society--a subordination exemplified in medieval marriages based on convention rather than, like Parzival's, on love:

... Wolfram solved the spiritual problem of his century first by
setting the ideal of love above marriage and, simultaneously, the
ideal of an indissoluble marriage beyond love .... As far as I know, he
was the first poet in the world to put forward seriously this socially
explosive ideal of marriage, which has become today, however, the
romantic norm of the West, resisted and even despised in the Orient
as anarchic, immoral, and insane. For through it are transcended the
primitive, ancient, and Oriental orders of tribal and family marriage,
where social, political, and economic considerations prevail over
personal and romantic, and where the unfolding personality (which in
the lore of this revelation is the flower of human life) is bound back,
cropped and trained to the interests of a group. (1968:567-568)[34]

In fact, in all but volume one of *Masks* Campbell ignores the social origin as
well as function of myth. He considers mythology an autonomous set of beliefs. To
be sure, in *Masks: Occidental* he ascribes the difference, or seeming difference,
between the mythology of the East and that of the West to differing social
organizations: matriarchy and patriarchy. But he never examines any societies
themselves, only the beliefs expressed in their myths. Indeed, it is finally not clear
whether for Campbell myth reflects society or vice versa. In *Masks: Oriental*
Campbell roots the mythological differences in differing beliefs themselves: the
Eastern belief in the oneness of all things and the Western belief in the uniqueness
of all things. The relationship between the individual and society is simply a
consequence of the relationship between the individual and the cosmos. Only in
Masks: Primitive does Campbell really link mythological differences to the
environment, but even there the environment is economic rather than social.
Moreover, the differing beliefs that myths express are so abstract and metaphysical
as to transcend any possible economic roots.

In order to distinguish the secular, individualist, later Western outlook from the
prior religious, collectivist one, Campbell argues that it represents the resurfacing of
a pagan, pre-Christian tradition that Christianity had vainly tried to eradicate.
Campbell labels this tradition distinctively European and identifies it with one of the
strains forming the West: the strain composed of Greeks, Romans, Celts, and
Germans.[35] The twelfth century represents the beginning of the continuing revolt
by this secular, individualist strain against the religious, collectivist "Levantine"
one, composed of Jews, Muslims, and above all Christians:

The great period of the breakthrough of the native European spirit
against the imposed authority of decisions made by a lot of Levantine
bishops at the Councils of Nicaea, Constantinople, Ephesus, and
Chalcedon (fourth to eighth centuries A.D.), occurred in the twelfth
and thirteenth centuries .... As I see it, this breakthrough followed as
the consequence of the courage of an increasing number of people of
great stature to credit their own experience and to live by it against
the dictates of authority. (1969:208)

Because Campbell considers *Tristan* and *Parzival* the two greatest exemplars of this revolt, he argues that they constitute a rejection of Christianity, which means of otherworldly, institutionalized religion, in favor of worldly, individualistic experience:

> Though himself probably a cleric, and certainly learned in theology, Gottfried is openly disdainful of current Christian doctrines.... Chiefly, Gottfried's inspiration had sprung from his recognition in the Celtic legend ... [of] an order of poetic imagery congenial to his own mode of experience. It was a legend rooted, like all Arthurian romance, in the most ancient native European mythological tradition--that of the old megalithic, bronze-age goddess of many names .... The Grail legend, also, had sprung from that pagan base.... [I]n rejecting absolutely the authority of the Church, these lovers and poets returned consciously and conscientiously to an earlier, pre-Christian, native European order of conscience, wherein the immanence of divinity was recognized in nature and its productions .... (1969:216-217, 222)

When, finally, Campbell says that the secular individualism introduced by courtly love fully affirms rather than, as before, rejects the everyday world--the change to which the phrase "secularization of the sacred" refers--it is hard to reconcile this claim with his heretofore relentless praise of the East for accomplishing exactly this end, which is that of the radical variety of radical monism:

> ... this, after all, is the leading lesson of Arthurian romance in general. Within its fold the gods and goddesses of other days have become [human] knights and ladies, hermits and kings of this world, their dwellings castles; and the adventures, largely magical, are of the magic rather of poetry than of traditional religion, not so much miracles of God as signs of an unfolding dimension of nature .... (1968:566)

Like Jung, Campbell considers distinctively later Western man to be not the average person of the period but the exception. Campbell is unabashedly elitist. For him, as for Jung, only the few are sensitive to the breakdown of tradition. Most persons living even today cling obliviously to traditional religion and so traditional myths, which therefore continue to work for them. As Campbell says elsewhere, "The traditional myths--Christian and otherwise--still offer support for large numbers of people in our society."[36] It is only an elite who seek new myths.

NOTES

1 Campbell elsewhere puts the point perhaps more clearly: "Whenever the social structuring of the unconscious is dissolved, the individual has to take a heroic journey and go within to find new forms" (interview with Sam Keen in Keen, *Voices and Visions* [New York: Harper and Row, 1974], 740).

2 *Ibid.*, 77. See also *ibid.*, 78-79.

3 On *Tristan* see Campbell 1968:42-46, 65-67, 175-256; 1973:160-165.

4 See also Campbell 1973:ch. 8.

5 On the Grail legend see Campbell 1968:405-570; 1969:209-222; 1973:166-171; "Indian Reflections in the Castle of the Grail," in *The Celtic Consciousness*, ed. Robert O'Driscoll (New York: Braziller, 1982), 3-30; introduction to Helen Diner, *Mothers and Amazons*, ed. and tr. John Philip Lundin (New York: Julian, 1965), vii. For a summary of the versions see John Matthews, *The Grail* (New York: Crossroad, 1981).

6 It is this version Thomas Malory translates in his *Le Morte D'Arthur.*

7 On the Parzival version as pre-Christian and Celtic see Campbell 1969:217-222; introduction to Diner, vii.

8 On Catharism see Steven Runciman, *The Medieval Manichee* (Cambridge, England: Cambridge University, 1947), ch. 4.

9 On Weston see Campbell 1968:406-407, 457-458; introduction to Diner, vii.

10 Jessie L. Weston, *From Ritual to Romance* (Garden City, NY: Doubleday Anchor, 1957), 203.

11 *Ibid.*, ch. 11. Furthermore, Weston derives her views from A. E. Waite, W. B. Yeats, and other members of the ascetic Hermetic Order of the Golden Dawn.

12 Campbell, introduction to Diner, vii.

13 Campbell, "Indian Reflections in the Castle of the Grail," 16-17.

14 In *Masks* Campbell associates only *Tristan*, not *Parzival*, with Gnosticism, and, as quoted, associates it with opposition to Gnosticism.

15 See also Campbell, "Contransmagnificandjewbangtantiality," *Studies in the Literary Imagination*, 3 (October 1970), 7. On the difference between medieval Gnostics and the East see Runciman, appendix IV.

[16] On Mann see Campbell 1968:38-40, 308-333, 358-364, 366-367, 374-383, 636-645, 658-662; "Erotic Irony and Mythic Forms in the Art of Thomas Mann," *Boston University Journal*, 24 (1976), 10-27.

[17] On Joyce see Campbell 1968:38-40, 257-262, 274-277, 280-281, 283-285, 338-339, 364-373, 635-636, 639-642, 656-665; *A Skeleton Key to Finnegans Wake* (with Henry Morton Robinson) (New York: Harcourt, Brace, 1944); "Finnegan the Wake," *Chimera*, 4 (Spring 1946), 63-80; "Contransmagnificand-jewbangtantiality," 3-18. On both see Campbell, "Mythological Themes in Creative Literature and Art," in *Myths, Dreams, and Religion*, ed. Campbell (New York: Dutton, 1970), 175; "The Occult in Myth and Literature," in *Literature and the Occult*, ed. Luanne Frank (Arlington: University of Texas at Arlington, 1977), 16-17.

[18] Yet at the same time Settembrini's escape from the everyday world to the sanitorium, where talk takes the place of living, itself represents rejection of the world and so radical dualism.

[19] On Joyce as a radical monist see also Campbell, "Contransmagnificandjew-bangtantiality," 607.

[20] See Campbell 1969:chs. 5 ("The Symbol without Meaning"), 6 ("The Secularization of the Sacred"); 1973:chs. 4 ("The Separation of East and West"), 5 ("The Confrontation of East and West in Religion").

[21] As one commentator says of Campbell's earlier view of the individual, "He [Campbell] accordingly sees the disintegration of mythology as an underlying principle of social morality and of the collective sense of beauty, a disintegration insensibly brought about by 'the individual.' Ambivalent though he is throughout in his attitude toward the individual, there is no doubt that Campbell generally sees the individual as a selfish, arrogant egomaniac" (A. J. Prats, "The Individual, the World, and the Life of Myth in *Fellini Satyricon*," *South Atlantic Bulletin*, 44 [1979], 45.

[22] See also Campbell, interview with Keen, 77-81.

[23] See, for example, Campbell 1969:ch. 6.

[24] Sam Keen, interview with Campbell, 71.

[25] Florence Sandler and Darrell Reeck, "The Masks of Joseph Campbell," *Religion*, 11 (January 1981), 1-20.

[26] Campbell, "The Symbol without Meaning," *Eranos-Jahrbücher*, 26 (1957), 415-476. Reprinted in partially revised form in Campbell 1969:ch. 5.

[27] Campbell, "The Secularization of the Sacred," in *The Religious Situation*, vol. 1 (1968), ed. Donald R. Cutler (Boston: Beacon, 1968), ch. 17. Reprinted in Campbell 1969:ch. 6.

[28] In Campbell 1973:ch. 4, which was first delivered as a lecture in 1961, Campbell is pro-Western but not anti-Eastern in particular. Rather, he opposes everything that is different from the later West: primitives and the earlier West as well as the East.

[29] See also Campbell 1962:4, 168.

[30] Since, in *Masks: Occidental*, Campbell says on the one hand that Eastern matriarchy preceded Western patriarchy and on the other hand that primitive planting corresponds to the East and primitive hunting to the West, is he therefore saying, contrary to *Masks: Primitive*, that primitive planting, which he also considers matriarchal, preceded rather than succeeded primitive hunting, which he considers matriarchal?

[31] For a brief anticipation of this parallel see Campbell 1959:281.

[32] See, for example, Campbell's definition of myth in his "Folkloristic Commentary" to *Grimm's Fairy Tales*, ed. Josef Scharl, tr. Margaret Hunt, rev. James Stern (New York: Pantheon, 1944): "religious recitations conceived as symbolic of the play of Eternity in Time" (841).

[33] Indeed, Richard Chase faults Campbell in *Hero* for espousing the absorption of the individual in the group: see Chase, review of *Hero*, *Nation*, 169 (July 2, 1949), 17; Chase, *Democratic Vista* (Garden City, NY: Doubleday Anchor, 1958), 83.

[34] Whether a secular mythology can even fulfill this social function will be considered in ch. 10, p. 121.

[35] See Campbell 1969:215.

[36] Campbell, interview with Keen, 78. But see Campbell 1972:8-9 (quoted in the conclusion, p. 137), where he says that the modern West is in chaos because science has undone traditional religion and so traditional myths.

Chapter Seven

THE MYTHIC IMAGE
and the
HISTORICAL ATLAS OF WORLD MYTHOLOGY

Both *The Mythic Image* and the *Historical Atlas of World Mythology* are pictorial accompaniments to Campbell's earlier works. *The Mythic Image*, which corresponds to no specific earlier work, seems far more radical than the *Atlas*, which is the accompaniment to, specifically, part three of *Masks: Primitive*. Where the *Atlas* is a combination of texts and pictures, *The Mythic Image* is largely a set of pictures themselves. For the principal theme in the book is that only pictures, not words, can capture the true meaning of myth. Because the *Atlas*, by contrast, combines both, presumably both elucidate the meaning of myth. Yet in an interview Campbell, referring to the *Atlas*, nearly says otherwise:

> Mythology is primarily image, and the discourse of myth is an amplification of the meaning of image. When you write, I don't care how much poetic and mystical imagination you put into it, it doesn't have the impact of a picture. In this book, I have the text and relevant picture on the same page.[1]

THE MYTHIC IMAGE

In several respects *The Mythic Image* marks a return to *Hero*. First and foremost, Campbell no longer concerns himself with the differences among myths but seeks only the similarities. Where in *Masks* he stresses at least the seeming, if not the real, differences between hunting and planting myths, between Western and Eastern myths, and between all other and later Western myths, now, as in *Hero*, he deems all myths the same. Moreover, they are the same not just underneath, as Campbell has to argue in *Masks*, but on the surface. To be sure, Campbell never denies even here that differences exist. In fact, he goes so far as to say that in them rather than in the similarities the "fascination resides" (1974:11). But he then states that "it has been my leading thought in the present work to let sound the one accord through all its ranges of historic transformation, not allowing local features to obscure the everlasting themes ..." (1974:11-12).

Second, where in *Masks* Campbell interprets myths almost entirely metaphysically, in *The Mythic Image*, as again in *Hero*, he interprets them psychologically as well. To use his new terms, he again interprets myths "microcosmically" as well as "macrocosmically" (1974:221).

Whenever Campbell interprets myth psychologically, he compares myths with dreams. In other works he does so to argue only that both emanate from the unconscious,[2] in which case their true meaning, not to say origin and function, is psychological, even if also metaphysical. In *The Mythic Image* Campbell not merely interprets both myths and dreams psychologically but interprets myths as dream-like themselves. Where, in other works, Campbell distinguishes myths from dreams on the grounds that myths are the "consciously controlled" rather than "spontaneous products" (1949:256) of the unconscious,[3] now he views myths themselves as raw, spontaneous outpourings of the unconscious. Where, in other works, Campbell interprets myth as the formal arrangement of images in a logical, narrative sequence, now he sees it as a series of disparate images themselves. Not coincidentally, he no longer discusses whole myths, only discrete images.[4]

Where, in other works, myths abide by the ordinary rules of logic, now they heed their own, dream-like logic. Where elsewhere myths preach the logical reconciliation of only apparent opposites, now they espouse a paradoxical reconciliation of real opposites. In so doing, they violate the law of noncontradiction, according to which A and not-A, be they man and god or matter and immateriality, cannot be the same:

> However, as a mythological image transcending the popular notion of
> an absolute dichotomy of nature and spirit (A is not not-A: man is
> not God), it makes once again the point that had already been made
> (though canonically disregarded) in the doctrine of the Incarnation,
> where in the person of Jesus not only was the idea of the absolute
> distinction of the opposed terms God and man refuted, but the point
> was also made that one should realize, like Jesus, this coincidence
> of opposites as the ultimate truth and substance of oneself ....
> (1974:62)[5]

Where, in other works, myths are to be interpreted, now they, like dreams, are only to be experienced.[6] Interpretation itself now proves part of only the ordinary, waking world. In claiming to interpret dreams and myths alike, both Freud and Jung must therefore have missed the point. To transcend the bounds of the everyday, waking world, with which Campbell associates not only logic but also language, he now resorts to pictures, which supplement and no doubt finally replace words.

In other works Campbell uses Western psychology--Freud and Jung--to "psychologize" myths. Now he employs Eastern psychology: Kundalini yoga,[7] which underlies the beliefs of both Hinduism and Buddhism. As Campbell summarizes its precepts:

> The basic thesis of the so-called Kundalini yoga system elucidated in this fundamental work is that there are six plus one--i.e., seven-- psychological centers distributed up the body, from its base to the crown of the head, which can, through yoga, be successively activated and so caused to release ever higher realizations of spiritual consciousness and bliss. These are known as "lotuses," *padmas*, or as *chakras*, "wheels," and are to be thought of as normally hanging limp. However, when touched and activated by a rising spiritual center called the Kundalini, which can be made to ascend through a mystic channel up the middle of the spine, they awaken to life and shine. The name of this power, *kundalini*, "the coiled one," is a feminine Sanskrit noun, here referring to the idea of a coiled serpent, to be thought of as sleeping in the lowest of the seven body centers. (1973: 110)

The aim is to advance from the first level to the seventh by the transformation, or sublimation, of spiritual energy. Not to advance is to become fixated. Each chakra, or level of consciousness, corresponds to a certain kind of myth. At level one, which lies midway between the genitals and the anus, a person takes a wholly material view of himself and the world. He believes in only "hard facts." He denies the existence of a psyche and believes in the sheer conditioning of man by the environment. Behaviorist psychology clearly lies here. As Campbell describes the outlook: "There is on this plane no zeal for life, no explicit impulse to expand [i.e., to grow]. There is simply a lethargic avidity in hanging on to [everyday] existence ..." (1974:341). Kundalini yoga thus becomes a means of interpreting not only myths but interpretations of myths--Campbell's seeming dismissal of interpretation as inappropriate for myth somehow aside.

At level two, that of the genitals, there is a psyche, but it is composed of entirely material drives--the sexual one above all. Myths here describe the direct or indirect satisfaction of that drive. Freudian psychology obviously falls here:

> When the Kundalini is active at this level, the whole aim of life is in sex. Not only is every thought and act sexually motivated, either as a means toward sexual ends or as a compensating sublimation of frustrated sexual zeal, but everything seen and heard is interpreted compulsively, both consciously and unconsciously, as symbolic of sexual themes. (1974:345)

At level three, that of the navel, the psyche is composed of a less tangible and more assertive, hence more creative drive: the drive for power, though power still takes material form. "Here the energy turns to violence and its aim is to consume, to master, to turn the world into oneself and one's own" (1974:350). The psychology of Alfred Adler lies here.

The satisfactions of the first three levels are not only material but also external. They deal with man's relationship to the external world:

> Now all three of these lower chakras are of the modes of man's living in the world in his naive state, outward turned: the modes of the lovers, the fighters, the builders, the accomplishers. Joys and sorrows on these levels are functions of achievements in the world "out there": what people think of one, what has been gained, what lost. (1974: 356)

By contrast, levels four to seven deal with man's relationship to the internal world: the world of the psyche. Levels two and three do presuppose a psyche, but the satisfaction of it is external. From level four on the satisfaction is internal. The shift from the first three levels to the last four is, in Jung's terms, the shift from the first half of life to the second.

At level four one merely discovers, or rediscovers, the inner world. In so doing, he abandons the outer world. He does not yet connect the two. Jung's psychology, Campbell says elsewhere, lies here: in the sheer rediscovery of the inner world.[8] Doubtless the reason is that even though Jung certainly does insist on the reconnection of the inner world with the outer one, he does not preach their mystical fusion. As noted,[9] Jung seeks a harmony between the two but still a distinction between them. For Campbell, anything short of fusion likely constitutes less than even a reconnection.

The difference between the sixth and the seventh levels, both of them mystical, is that at the sixth level one is still conscious of himself vis-à-vis the world, inner and outer alike. Only at the seventh level does he lose all self-consciousness and become one with all things. Not only does he thereby become--better, prove to be-- identical with both inner and outer worlds, but they prove to be identical with each other. Kundalini yoga here certainly goes contrary to Jung, for whom the fusion of outer with inner, of ego with unconscious, would yield the sheer dissolution of the ego rather than a higher combination of it and the unconscious. The result, in Jungian terms, would be inflation and, ultimately, psychosis.[10]

For Campbell, the result is perfection. It is the realization of the radical brand of radical monism: the fusion of all opposites into a single, higher unity. In *Hero* and half the time in *Masks* the attainment of that unity is the goal of all myths. In *The Mythic Image* it turns out to be the goal of just the highest category of myths, though likely only because the creators of lesser categories have yet to ascend to higher levels of consciousness. For Campbell, the ultimate message of myth is always the same: unity. Psychologically, the unity is of the ego with the unconscious. Metaphysically, it is of the individual with the cosmos and of all cosmic domains with one another. Psychologically, the yogi ascends through the levels of his own consciousness. Metaphysically, he ascends through the levels of the cosmos.

HISTORICAL ATLAS OF WORLD MYTHOLOGY

Volume one of the *Atlas* deals entirely with primitive hunters and thereby corresponds to part three of volume one of *Masks*. Volume two of the *Altas*, which will deal with primitive planters, will correspond to part two of volume one of *Masks*.

In the *Atlas*, as in *Masks*, geography determines economics, which determines myth. Primitives who live on the plains become hunters and view the world accordingly:

> The landscape of the "Great Hunt," typically, was of a spreading plain, cleanly bounded by a circular horizon, with the great blue dome of an exalting heaven above, where hawks and eagles hovered and the blazing sun passed daily; becoming dark by night, star-filled, and with the moon there, waning and waxing. The essential food supply was of the multitudinous grazing herds, brought in by the males of the community following dangerous physical encounters. And the ceremonial life was addressed largely to the ends of a covenant with the animals, of reconciliation, veneration, and assurance that in return for the beasts' unremitting offering of themselves as willing victims, their life-blood should be given back in a sacred way to the earth, the mother of all, for rebirth. (1983:9)

Primitives who live in the jungle become farmers and likewise view the world accordingly:

> In contrast, the environment of jungle tribes is of a dense and mighty foliage, the trunks and branches of prodigious trees; no horizon; no dome of the sky; but above, a ceiling of leaves populated by screeching birds, and underfoot a rough leafage, beneath which may lurk scorpions and lethal fangs. Out of the rot of fallen wood and leaves, fresh sprouts arise--from which the lesson learned appears to have been that from death springs life, out of death, new birth; and the grim conclusion drawn was that the way to increase life is to increase death. Accordingly, there has been endemic to the entire equatorial belt of this globe what can be described only as a frenzy of sacrifice, vegetable, animal, and human .... (1983:9-10)

Myths express the differing experiences of each group.

As in *Masks*, so here: Campbell associates hunters with male rule, male gods, tricksters, and shamans. As in *Masks*, so here as well: Campbell characterizes hunting in contradictory ways. It means death on the one hand but immortality on the other, killing on the one hand but self-sacrifice on the other, self-centered individuality on the one hand but mystical unity on the other:

> And every hunter, in his sacrificial killing, is in the role of Kaggen

himself, identified with the animal of his kill and at the same time
guilty, as the god is guilty, with the primordial guilt of life that lives
on life. (1983:93)[11]

Once again, Campbell is thus arguing that hunters and planters, like Westerners
and Easterners, are somehow at once different and the same. On the one hand he
argues that the experiences, and so the myths, of hunters are the opposite of those
of planters:

These, then, are two contrary orders of life, determinant of the life-
styles, mythologies, and rites of the most primitive peoples known:
one, of the widespreading animal plains, the other of the sheltering
forest. They were not arrived at by reason, but are grounded in
fundamental experiences .... (1983:112)

On the other hand Campbell argues that the experiences, and so the myths, of
hunters and planters are really, like those of all other humans, basically the same:

Significant differences will be evident between the primary
Paleolithic and recent ethnological materials; also, between the
mythologies of hunting, foraging, planting, and herding tribes, no less
than between those, generally, of the nonliterate and literate
traditions. Nevertheless, through all these contrasts ... there will be
recognizable, also, a constellation of permanent, archetypal themes
and motifs, which are as intrinsic to human life and thought as are
the ribs, vertebrae, and cranial parts to our anatomy. (1983:42)[12]

To the extent that primitive hunters are really no different from primitive
planters the fundamental message of their myths is, for Campbell, the fundamental
message of all other myths: that everything is ultimately one. Indeed, as Campbell
says of all the volumes that will compose his *Atlas*, "The unfolding through time of
all things from one is the simple message, finally, of every one of the creation
myths reproduced in the pages of these volumes ..." (1983:10).

Though Campbell scorns them throughout his writings, in his *Atlas* he is
especially contemptuous of "theologians." But where elsewhere he condemns them
for interpreting myths literally and historically rather than symbolically and
psychologically, now he berates them for interpreting myths at all. As part of his
stress on the spontaneousness of mythology, Campbell maintains that myths
express raw, unfiltered experience, which theologians then artificially "interpret."
Indeed, Campbell now argues for comparativism on the grounds that, as others
often say of mystical experience, there is a single, universal mythic experience or
set of experiences on which theologians, who are invariably Western, impose
interpretations to fit the convictions of their specific religions:

Whether either Bunjil of the Kurnai or the Yahweh specifically of
Genesis 2 and 3 is actually equivalent to the "idea of God" of any

respectable metaphysician today is a nice question for theologians; but in any case, the recognized sharing of such mythic themes by the simplest known religions with some of those we think of as the most advanced would seem, at least, to say something about the constancy of mythological archetypes. Whether interpreted theologically as supernatural revelations, or naturally as effects of the mind, they exist, endure, and undergo significant transformations on a plane little affected, apparently, by any readily identifiable sociological or philosophical influences. (1983:139)[13]

Eastern theologians, if theologians they are, know that their gods and heroes are mere symbols of a universal god and hero rather than the symbolized themselves.

NOTES

[1] Campbell, interview with Garry Abrams, "World Mythology in Modern Vogue," *Los Angeles Times*, 103 (January 13, 1984), section V, 2.

[2] See, for example, Campbell 1949:4; 1951:335; 1969:32-33.

[3] Richard Chase's criticism of *Hero* (review of *Hero, Nation* 169 [July 2, 1949], 18) for viewing myth as a spontaneous, psychological product rather than a conscious, artistic one--as a dream rather than literature--is therefore misplaced.

[4] Campbell systematically fails to make clear whether those images are, as I assume, archetypes themselves or only symbols expressing them: see ch. 9, pp. 106-107.

[5] See also Campbell 1974:58, 305-478.

[6] Cf. Campbell 1983:112, 139.

[7] On Kundalini yoga see Campbell 1974:278-281, 303-305, 330-387; 1973:109-116; "Seven Levels of Consciousness," *Psychology Today*, 9 (December 1975), 77-78; "The Interpretation of Symbolic Forms," in *The Binding of Prometheus*, eds. Marjorie W. McCune and others (Lewisburg, PA: Bucknell University, 1980), 50-58; "Masks of Oriental Gods: Symbolism of Kundalini Yoga," in *Literature of Belief*, ed. Neal E. Lambert (Salt Lake City, UT: Brigham Young University, 1981), ch. 6, all but the first few pages of which are a reprinting of *The Mythic Image*, 330-381.

[8] See Campbell, "Seven Levels of Consciousness," 78. In neither *The Mythic Image* nor *Myths to Live By* does Campbell associate Jung with this level or any other.

[9] See ch. 1, p. 8; ch. 2, pp. 20-23.

[10] For Jung's view of Kundalini yoga see Jung, "Psychological Commentary on Kundalini Yoga" (from the Notes of Mary Foote), *Spring* (1975) 1-32; (1976) 1-31. See also Harold Coward, *Jung and Eastern Thought* (Albany: State University of New York, 1985), ch. 6.

[11] See also Campbell 1983:76, 79, 148, 152.

[12] See also Campbell 1983:73, 79, where, to complicate the issue, he compares hunting myths with Eastern ones.

[13] See also Campbell 1983:112, where, as quoted, he ascribes the differences between hunters and planters to actual experience rather than reflection.

Chapter Eight

CAMPBELL AS A COMPARATIVIST

Like any other class of phenomena, myth is approachable as either a particular or a universal. One can analyze a myth either as a specific myth--as the *Theogony* rather than the *Enuma Elish*--or as an instance of a class--the class of creation myths, hero myths, or all myths. One can ask either what distinguishes one myth from any other or what that myth shares with all others.

The two approaches to myth, as to other phenomena, seem distinct and therefore compatible. They seem to be asking different questions: what makes myths different and what makes them similar?

To take an analogy, one can be interested in Socrates either as Socrates or as a member of the class of philosophers, Greeks, or human beings. If one is interested in Socrates as Socrates, one looks for exactly those qualities that distinguish him from other philosophers, Greeks, and human beings. If one is interested in Socrates as a philosopher, a Greek, or a human being, one looks for those qualities that he shares with others in the class. To single out Socrates' unique characteristics--for example, his skepticism--is not to deny his common ones but only to ignore them as irrelevant. Conversely, to focus on those characteristics that Socrates shares with others--for example, two arms and two legs--is only to ignore, not deny, the ones that he alone possesses.

Yet in the case of myth, as in the cases of other human phenomena, the two approaches, or at least their proponents, clash. Each side declares its approach not just necessary for understanding myth but sufficient. Each denies not the compatibility but the importance of the other. Neither, to be sure, assumes that it can wholly encompass the other. Particularists concede that even after all the differences have been explicated, some similarities remain: exactly those qualities that make any myth a myth. Particularists simply dismiss those similarities as too general to be important. Universalists, for their part, grant that even after all possible similarities have been explicated, differences remain: those qualities that make any two myths distinct. But they in turn reject those differences as trivial.

A COMPARISON OF TWO HERO MYTHS

A comparison of the myths about two ancient heroes, the Greek Odysseus and the Roman Aeneas, may illustrate the difference between particularists and universalists.

Both Odysseus and Aeneas undertake a series of dangerous journeys to distant places. By Campbell's criteria, the two are heroic because they succeed where others would either fail or never try.

Particularists, however, would immediately cite the differences. Odysseus, they would note, is seeking to return home to Ithaca, which he left for the Trojan War. Aeneas, by contrast, is seeking a new home. His old home, Troy, has been razed by the Greeks. Odysseus is seeking to re-establish himself as husband, father, and ruler. Having lost his wife, his father, and his country, Aeneas is seeking to establish a new family and nation. Where Odysseus finally returns home, Aeneas, breaking with Campbell's scheme, finally finds a new one.

Odysseus wants to return home for his own sake. By contrast, Aeneas leaves Troy only because he is commanded to go. Duty, not self-interest, motivates him. Odysseus might have been acting selflessly in leaving for Troy in the first place, but it is Aeneas, not Odysseus, who is selfless in leaving it now. He would have wished either to die at Troy during the fighting or to rebuild it on its ruins.

At the same time Odysseus is initially not so eager to return home promptly. He insists on seeing the world in the process. It is out of curiosity that he meets the Cyclops. His crew must beseech him to forsake Circe. Though he declines Calypso's offer of immortality in exchange for remaining with her, she does tempt him. With her offer of wealth and power Nausicaa tempts him to stay, too. Even if most of the world he encounters is barbaric, much of it is most alluring. Returning home requires resolve, as Campbell himself would stress.

With Aeneas, however, venturing forth in the first place requires resolve. Both his mother, Venus, and his dead wife, Creusa, must urge him to go. Once he leaves, his father, his mother, and other gods must prod him to continue his journey. Dido proves the strongest tempter--not, however, because she, like Calypso, offers him immortality in a supernatural world but, on the contrary, because she offers him the human domesticity that he was forced to abandon at Troy.

In the fashion of Campbell's pattern, Odysseus' adventures take him to a strange, barbaric, supernatural realm filled with monsters and other dangers. Though Aeneas encounters a few supernatural entities--the Harpies, the Cyclopes, and Scylla and Charybdis--he encounters largely human foe. Once both reach their destinations, they must still defeat enemies: the suitors in the case of Odysseus, the Latins in the case of Aeneas. Yet even the suitors, while human, represent a continuation of the barbarism that Odysseus had encountered worldwide. By contrast, Aeneas' enemies are much less barbaric.

Odysseus and Aeneas share above all a descent to the underworld. As a descent from the world of the living to that of the dead and back, the trek is doubtless the most extraordinary feat for both. But, again, particularists would note the differences. From his descent Odysseus learns his own personal destiny. From his descent Aeneas learns the destiny of his whole people. If Odysseus is transformed by his visit, the transformation takes the form not of spurring him homeward but, in the wake of the mere shadowy existence he witnesses in Hades, of valuing life. By contrast, Aeneas' undeniable transformation takes the form of strengthening his determination to proceed to Italy. Odysseus now treasures his old home even more. Aeneas is at last able to break with his.

Odysseus lands home alone, having lost all of his crew. In no small part he is heroic because he alone survives. Aeneas lands with virtually all of his followers save for those he left to establish a colony in Sicily. He is heroic because he makes it to Italy with his followers. Had he alone survived, he would have been considerably less heroic.

Odysseus' return is an entirely personal triumph; Aeneas', that of a whole people. Odysseus is the ruler of one small kingdom within Greece, and even it he scarcely founded. Aeneas is the founder of a future civilization. In returning, Odysseus, contrary to Campbell's scheme, bestows no "boon" on his fellow Greeks or even Ithacans. The future of neither Greece nor even Ithaca rests with him. By contrast, Aeneas comes to Italy precisely to bestow the greatest possible boon on his people: the founding of the greatest empire in the world.

Odysseus' success stems primarily from his own cunning and resourcefulness. Aeneas' stems from divine aid. Though Odysseus, too, has divine help, he is far more independent than Aeneas.

Finally, Vergil is clearly writing to present a Roman alternative to Homer's Greek heroism. His revulsion for Odysseus, whom he portrays as ruthless and treacherous, underscores the difference. Vergil's likely questioning of the worth of even Aeneas' feat puts his view of heroism even farther afield of Homer's.

Against comparativists, particularists would say in sum that even when the adventures of Odysseus and Aeneas follow Campbell's heroic pattern, that pattern provides only an outline to be filled in differently by each mythmaker. The pattern is like an archetype for Jung: its meaning comes from the particular form it takes in any individual case. In response, comparativists would say that the common fact of heroism, as sketched by Campbell's pattern, far outweighs the idiosyncrasies of each case.

Rather than try to resolve what is perhaps an unresolvable issue, it may be more useful to try to determine how staunch a comparativist Campbell really is. Does Campbell in fact believe, as an uncompromising comparativist would, that the similarities among myths are not just necessary but sufficient to explain the origin and function of a myth and to interpret its meaning?

CAMPBELL'S RECOGNITION OF DIFFERENCES

Certainly Campbell never denies differences. He recognizes differences not only between one category of myth and another--for example, between creation and hero myths--but also between one individual myth and another. Even his hero pattern, which is by far his most elaborate, is exceedingly flexible. The hero need only leave the everyday world for a supernatural one, encounter female and male gods, and return victoriously with some power for his fellow man. Though the hero must be a male adult, he can be young or old, human or divine, rich or poor, king or commoner. How and why he ventures forth, how he gains entry to the new world, what boon he secures, how he secures it, and how he returns home are all open-ended:

> The mythological hero, setting forth from his commonday hut or castle, is lured, carried away, or else voluntarily proceeds, to the threshold of adventure. There he encounters a shadow presence that guards the passage. The hero may defeat or conciliate this power and go alive into the kingdom of the dark (brother-battle, dragon-battle; offering, charm), or be slain by the opponent and descend in death (dismemberment, crucifixion). Beyond the threshold, then, the hero journeys through a world of unfamiliar yet strangely intimate forces, some of which severely threaten him (tests), some of which give magical aid (helpers). When he arrives at the nadir of the mythological round, he undergoes a supreme ordeal and gains his reward. The triumph may be represented as the hero's sexual union with the goddess-mother of the world (sacred marriage), his recognition by the father-creator (father atonement), his own divinization (apotheosis) .... The final work is that of the return. If the powers have blessed the hero, he now sets forth under their protection (emissary); if not, he flees and is pursued (transformation flight, obstacle flight). (1949:245-246)

Campbell himself stresses the variety: "The changes rung on the simple scale of the monograph defy description" (1949:246).[1] Hero myths sometimes focus on only one or two elements of the pattern, sometimes fuse elements, and sometimes duplicate elements (1949:246).

Furthermore, Campbell grants that a mythic pattern or archetype expresses itself only through a particular form, never pure: "... universals are never experienced in a pure state, abstracted from their locally conditioned ethnic applications" (1974:11).[2] Indeed, Campbell even says that in the differences, the "infinitely various metamorphoses" of universals, lies the "fascination" (1974:11).

Moreover, Campbell is prepared not merely to note differences but to explain their origin and function, whether or not to interpret their meaning. Because he explains the similarities psychologically, he must explain the differences nonpsychologically, which for him means socially and above all geographically. What Campbell says of initiation rites applies to myths, a term he in fact uses broadly to encompass rituals as well as stories:

> Hence, although the rites certainly have a psychological function and must be interpreted [i.e., explained] in terms of the general psychology of the human species, each local system itself has a long history behind it of a particular sort of social experience and cannot

be explained in general psychological terms. It has been closely adjusted to specific, geographically determined conditions of existence .... (1959:90-91)[3]

CAMPBELL'S STRESS ON SIMILARITIES

Yet even though Campbell thus acknowledges, if not stresses, the differences among myths, he finally dismisses them as trivial.[4] Myths, for him, are fundamentally the same: in origin, function, and meaning. They constitute a *"philosophia perennis* of the human race" (1973:264):

... in the face of the ubiquitous myth itself, its long persistence and the basic consistency of its lesson, all variations of detail must appear to be of only secondary moment; all finally conspire to inflect the single lesson.... [I]t is a story, therefore, which knows how to bend itself and reshape itself to the diverse needs of divers [sic] times and places; but there can be no doubt, it is one story. (1943:61-62)[5]

To cite an example, Campbell first stresses, not merely acknowledges, the differences in the myths about primordial androgynes. In Hinduism androgyny represents the mystical overriding of sexual, as of all other, distinctions. In Judaism androgyny symbolizes the pre-fallen state of man in Eden--division coming with the fall. In Aristophanes' speech in Plato's *Symposium* androgyny stands for the mystery of love: sexual attraction represents the reunification of the severed halves of man (1959:103-110). Yet after emphasizing these differences among the three mythologies, Campbell says:

If we now allow all three of these versions--the Hindu, the Hebrew, and the Greek--to supplement and play against one another in our minds, we shall certainly find it difficult to believe that they have not been derived from a single common tradition .... (1959:110)

Campbell's insistence on a common origin, while admittedly allowing for distinct meanings, surely makes the similarities paramount.

The reason that all myths are finally the same is that all mankind is. Like Freud and his follower Géza Róheim, Campbell stresses the "psychic unity" of man and faults the anthropologist Bronislaw Malinowski and other functionalists for being "dedicated to the proposition that mankind is not a species but an indefinitely variable dough, shaped by a self-creating demiurge, 'Society' " (1951:331).

THE ARGUMENT FOR COMPARATIVISM

What is Campbell's argument for the greater importance of similarities than differences? It is the sheer fact of similarities:

> Comparative cultural studies have now demonstrated beyond question
> that similar mythic tales are to be found in every quarter of this
> earth. When Cortes and his Catholic Spaniards arrived in Aztec
> Mexico, they immediately recognized in the local religion so many
> parallels to their own True Faith that they were hard put to explain
> the fact....There was a High God above all, who was beyond all human
> thought and imaging. There was even an incarnate Saviour, associated
> with a serpent, born of a virgin, who had died and was resurrected,
> one of whose symbols was a cross.... Modern scholarship,
> systematically comparing the myths and rites of mankind, has found
> just about everywhere legends of virgins giving birth to heroes who
> die and are resurrected. (1973:7-8)

So striking, for Campbell, are the similarities that the meaning, not to say the origin and function, of myth must lie in them.

Needless to say, particularists would demur. They might well deny the existence of the similarities. They would certainly deny their importance. They would argue that the differences count far more. They would argue that the sheer presence in even all myths of gods, virgins, heroes, saviors, death, and rebirth would beg, not answer, the key question: whether the archetypes mean the same in each case.

The appeal to similarities themselves is not just Campbell's ploy but the standard argument of all comparativists. For example, Edward Tylor argues that the similarities he finds in hero myths are too uniform to be coincidental, which for him means historical. They must therefore have a common source, which for him means a psychological one:

> Of all things, what mythologic work needs is breadth of knowledge
> and of handling. Interpretations made to suit a narrow view reveal
> their weakness when exposed to a wide one. See Herodotus
> rationalizing the story of the infant Cyrus, exposed and suckled by a
> bitch; he simply relates that the child was brought up by a herdsman's
> wife named Spakô, ... whence arose the fable that a real bitch rescued
> and fed him. So far so good--for a single case. But does the story of
> Romulus and Remus likewise record a real event, mystified in the self-same
> manner by a pun on a nurse's name, which happened to be a she-beast's?
> Did the Roman twins also really happen to be exposed, and brought up
> by a foster-mother who happened to be called Lupa?...[I]f we look properly
> into the matter, we find that these two stories are but specimens of a
> widespread mythic group, itself only a section of that far larger body of
> traditions in which exposed infants are saved to become national heroes.[6]

Lord Raglan argues the same. So common are the similarities he, too, finds in hero myths that they must have a common source, which for him means a ritualistic one:

> I doubt whether even the most fervent euhemerist would maintain that all these resemblances are mere coincidences; and if not, then three possibilities remain. The first is that all, or some, of the heroes were real persons whose stories were altered to make them conform to a ritual pattern; the second is that all, or some, of them were real persons in whose lives ritual played a predominant part; and the third [i.e., Raglan's view] is that they were all purely mythical [i.e., ritualistic].[7]

Like Tylor and especially Raglan, Campbell equates particularistic explanations with historical ones. But unlike them, he maintains that comparativist explanations render historical ones merely irrelevant, not incredible. On the one hand a hero myth hardly requires a historical hero behind it. On the other hand it does not preclude one:

> We may doubt whether such a scene ever actually took place. But that would not help us any; for we are concerned, at present, with problems of symbolism, not of historicity. We do not particularly care whether Rip van Winkle, Kamar al-Zaman, or Jesus Christ ever actually lived. (1949:230)[8]

Any theorist of myth, as a theorist, necessarily considers all myths basically the same. Theorists differ over what aspects of myth are the same: origin, function, or content. For Otto Rank, for example, the content as well as the origin and function of myth is the same: myth everywhere not only arises to release unconscious sexual wishes but, to do so, describes the realization of those wishes. Rank's, or Freud's, theory thus specifies the plot of myth. By contrast, for Malinowski[9] only the origin and function of myth are the same: myth everywhere arises to explain the origin of social and natural phenomena and thereby encourage the acceptance of them, but the explanations have no uniform plot.

For Campbell, the content as well as the origin and function of myth is the same--most clearly in the case of hero myths, where he provides a common plot, but in the cases of other myths as well. In *The Mythic Image* Campbell provides no common plot, but he does provide common motifs, or "images": sleep, dream, death, rebirth, child savior, virgin birth, world mountain, great goddess, cyclical time, axis mundi, primeval waters, serpent, sacrifice, awakening, and lotus. These images, or archetypes, are the counterparts to the archetypes that appear in hero myths: hero, call, journey, female and male gods, and return. But in *The Mythic Image* Campbell never interprets any of the archetypes, the way he does in *Hero*. He may therefore not be precluding differences in meaning from society to society.

At the outset of *Masks: Primitive* (1959:ch. 2) Campbell enumerates universal experiences that constitute less the images than the topics of myths: suffering, gravity, alternation of light and dark, division into male and female, birth, breast feeding, excreting, Oedipus and Electra Complexes, puberty, and old age. Though these shared topics constitute more of a common content than the sheer images of *The Mythic Image*, they do not add up to a common plot or a common meaning, which, as in *The Mythic Image*, may therefore vary from society to society.

Moreover, in much of the rest of *Masks*, as in all of the *Atlas*, Campbell wavers back and forth between stressing the differing experiences of peoples and stressing the similarities. When, then, Campbell says, as he does half the time, that hunters are at heart planters and Westerners at heart Easterners, he is coming close to saying that the meaning of all myths, which express those common experiences, is the same.

COMPARATIVISM AND SYMBOLISM

To say that the meaning of all myths is the same is not necessarily to make that meaning symbolic. Tylor, Raglan, and Vladimir Propp maintain that all hero myths have the same plot,[10] but none of them thereby deems the meaning of that plot symbolic. To qualify as a hero, a figure must, for all three, undertake the actions each prescribes, but none of the three says that in so doing the hero symbolizes something else. For all three, a hero is someone who literally, which does not mean historically, undertakes the adventures that his myth says he does.

By contrast, Campbell interprets heroism symbolically. Taken psychologically, a hero symbolizes the ego of man, and his adventures symbolize the ego's encounter with the unconscious. Taken metaphysically, a hero symbolizes the essence of man, and his adventures symbolize the encounter of that essence with the essence of the cosmos itself.

Because Tylor, Raglan, and Propp interpret hero myths comparatively yet literally, a comparativist interpretation need not entail a symbolic one. Campbell must therefore justify not only his comparativist analysis but, in addition, his symbolic one. To argue, as all comparativists do, that all heroes are fundamentally the same is to reduce individual heroes to mere instances of a class. It is not also to reduce that class to a symbol of something else.

Campbell misses the distinction. From the fact of similarities at the literal level--the fact of heroes worldwide undertaking the same kinds of adventures--he wrongly concludes not only that all heroes are the same--the differences being trivial--but also that they are symbolic--the literal similarities somehow canceling out one another. As he says of not just hero myths but myths in general:

> Traditionally, ... in the orthodoxies of popular faiths mythic beings
> and events are generally regarded and taught as facts; and this
> particularly in the Jewish and Christian spheres. There *was* an Exodus
> from Egypt; there *was* a Resurrection of Christ.... When these stories
> are interpreted, though, not as reports of historic fact, but as merely

imagined episodes projected onto history, and when they are recognized, then, as analogous to like projections produced elsewhere, ... the import becomes obvious; namely, that although false and to be rejected as accounts of physical history, such universally cherished figures of the mythic imagination must represent facts of the mind .... And whereas it must, of course, be the task of the historian, archaeologist, and prehistorian to show that the myths are as facts untrue--that there is no one Chosen People of God in this multiracial world, no Found Truth to which we all must bow, no One and Only True Church--it will be more and more, and with increasing urgency, the task of the psychologist and comparative mythologist ... to identify, analyze, and interpret the symbolized "facts of the mind ...." (1973:10-11)[11]

Now it may be true that no believer who realizes the existence of rival heroes worldwide can still accept his own alone--if, of course, he, like comparativists, is more impressed by the similarities than by the differences in the first place. But it by no means follows that the true meaning of heroism must therefore be symbolic. Nor does it follow that the true meaning of heroism for even the believer himself must therefore be symbolic. Surely his own particular hero can remain an instance of still literal, if now universal, heroism, as he would for Tylor, Raglan, and Propp.

Campbell can continue to claim that "whenever a myth has been taken literally its sense has been perverted" (1959:27), but he must do so as more than simply a comparativist. Indeed, if he is denying that no believer takes his own myths literally, surely that fact does not always stem from contact with the myths of other peoples. In that case Campbell must make his claim as other, not just more, than a comparativist.[12]

COMPARATIVISM AND HISTORICITY

If on the one hand Campbell, unlike Tylor and especially Raglan, never denies that a symbolic hero can also be a historical one, on the other hand he, unlike them as well, assumes that a literal *interpretation* of a hero or other myth is also a historical one. As the earlier quotation beginning "Traditionally" (1973:10-11) makes clear, Campbell takes for granted that to interpret myth literally is automatically to interpret it historically. Indeed, he abhors all historical interpretations because he assumes that the converse must somehow follow: that if literal interpretations are always historical, historical interpretations must always be literal.[13]

Campbell goes so far as to claim that myths get interpreted historically only once their symbolic meaning either has been lost or is no longer believed:

In the later stages of many mythologies, the key images hide like needles in great haystacks of secondary anecdote and rationalization;

for when a civilization has passed from a mythological to a secular
point of view, the older images are no longer felt or quite approved....
And in modern progressive Christianity the Christ--Incarnation of the
Logos and Redeemer of the World--is primarily a historical
personage, a harmless country wise man of the semi-oriental past,
who preached a benign doctrine of "do as you would be done by," yet
was executed as a criminal. His death is read as a splendid lesson in
integrity and fortitude. Wherever the poetry of myth is interpreted
as biography, history, or science, it is killed. The living images
become only remote facts of a distant time or sky. (1949:248-249)

NOTES

[1] Cf. Otto Rank ("The Myth of the Birth of the Hero," in his *The Myth of the Birth of the Hero and Other Writings*, ed. Philip Freund [New York: Vintage, 1959], 80-81), who notes variations in his pattern but downplays them, and Lord Raglan (*The Hero* [New York: Vintage, 1956], ch. 16), who ranks his hero myths by the degree to which they conform to his pattern but otherwise ignores the issue.

[2] See also Campbell 1959:32, 38, 130, 264, 461-462; 1983:8-9; "Myths from West to East," in Alexander Eliot, *Myths*, with contributions by Mircea Eliade and Campbell (New York: McGraw-Hill, 1976), 32.

[3] See also Campbell 1973:22.

[4] For a contrary view see William G. Doty, *Mythography* (Tuscaloosa: University of Alabama, 1986), 108-110. Doty praises Campbell exactly for combining the local with the universal. For a vigorous rejection of any opposition between the two approaches see Clifford Geertz, "The Impact of the Concept of Culture on the Concept of Man," in his *The Interpretation of Cultures* (New York: Basic, 1973), ch. 2.

[5] On myths as the same see also Campbell 1943: 59, 64; 1949:viii, 4, 21-22, 246-247; 1951:336; 1959:3, 4; 1983:42, 139.

[6] Edward B. Tylor, *Primitive Culture*, fifth ed. (New York: Harper Torchbooks, 1958, I (retitled *The Origins of Culture*), 281-282.

[7] Raglan, 186. Neither Rank nor Propp explicitly says that the similarities he finds among hero myths proves that the heart of the myths lies in them, but any preoccupation with similarities rather than differences surely presupposes the view.

[8] See also Campbell 1964:362; 1973:29, 262. For criticisms of Campbell's indifference to history see H. A. Reinhold, review of *Hero*, *Commonweal*, 50

(July 8, 1949), 322; Northrop Frye, review of *Masks: Occidental, New York Herald Tribune Book Week*, 1 (March 22, 1964), 6; M. C. D'Arcy, "God and Mythology," *Heythrop Journal*, 1 (April 1960), 95-104. For a criticism of Campbell's supposed insistence on history see Stanley Edgar Hyman, "Myth, Ritual, and Nonsense," *Kenyon Review*, 11 (Summer 1949), 471. Since Campbell in fact merely allows for a historical hero, not assumes one, Hyman's criticism is misplaced.

[9] See Bronislaw Malinowski, *Myth in Primitive Psychology* (London: Routledge and Kegan Paul, 1926).

[10] To be sure, Propp confines himself to Russian hero myths and, strictly, to fairy tales rather than to myths. Following Campbell, I am using the term hero myth broadly to cover all stories about heroes.

[11] See also Campbell 1973:24, 261-262; "The Interpretation of Symbolic Forms," in *The Binding of Prometheus*, eds. Marjorie W. McCune and others (Lewisburg, PA: Bucknell University, 1980), 43.

[12] For a criticism of Campbell's view that no believer takes his myths literally, whether or not historically, see Joseph Fontenrose, review of *The Flight of the Wild Gander, Western Humanities Review*, 24 (Winter 1970), 87. For a summary of literal and symbolic theories of myth see David Bidney, "Myth, Symbolism, and Truth," *Journal of American Folklore*, 68 (October-December 1955), 379-392.

[13] On myths as nonhistorical see Campbell 1949:248-249, 256, 321; 1964: 95, 124, 125, 137; 1969:ch. 3; 1973:chs. 1, 2, 12; "The Interpretation of Symbolic Forms," 36-43; "Masks of Oriental Gods: Symbolism of Kundalini Yoga," in *Literature of Belief*, ed. Neal E. Lambert (Salt Lake City, UT: Brigham Young University, 1981), 110-111; interview with Douglas Auchincloss, *Parabola*, 7 (Winter 1982), 80-81; interview with Sam Keen, in Keen, *Voices and Visions* (New York: Harper and Row, 1974), 75-76; interview with Lorraine Kisly, *Parabola*, 1 (Spring 1976), 75.

Chapter Nine

THE ORIGIN OF MYTH

Having committed himself to comparativism, how does Campbell account for the similarities he finds? There are only two possible explanations: independent invention and diffusion. Either every society on its own creates myth or else a single one does, from which it spreads to others. Independent invention and diffusion are only kinds of explanations, not specific explanations themselves. There can be social, political, economic, intellectual, and religious brands of independent invention. Similarly, diffusion can emanate from anywhere.

THE HERO WITH A THOUSAND FACES

Despite his modest claim in *Hero* (1949:39n43) that he is seeking only to *establish* the similarities among hero myths, Campbell is in fact seeking to account for them as well: "Why," he asks, "is mythology everywhere the same, beneath its varieties of costume?" (1949:4) His answer is psychological: myths are the same because the mind, which creates them, is. That answer is a case of independent invention: it assumes that the mind of all mankind is fundamentally the same, so that individuals everywhere will inevitably produce the same artifacts. The answer assumes the psychic unity of mankind.

On the one hand Campbell says repeatedly that myths arise spontaneously from the psyche, by which he means the unconscious: "For the symbols of mythology are not manufactured; they cannot be ordered, invented, or permanently suppressed. They are spontaneous productions of the psyche ..." (1949:4). Whether the contents of the unconscious are acquired, as for Freud, or inherited, as for Jung, Campbell considers at length in *Masks* but not at all in *Hero*, though he implies (1949:17) that they are inherited.

On the other hand Campbell distinguishes myths from dreams on exactly the grounds that myths are consciously created:

But if we are to grasp the full value of the materials, we must note

101

that myths are not exactly comparable to dream. Their figures
originate from the same sources--the unconscious wells of fantasy--
and their grammar is the same, but they are not the spontaneous
products of sleep. On the contrary, their patterns are consciously
controlled. (1949:256)

Moreover, Campbell continually maintains that ancients were aware of the true,
symbolic, psychological meaning of myths. Only moderns, who invariably read
myths literally, are not: "The old teachers knew what they were saying. Once we
have learned to read again their symbolic language, it requires no more than the
talent of an anthologist to let their teaching be heard" (1949:vii). How, then, can
Campbell still maintain that myths arise out of the unconscious?

Though Campbell never explains, he is presumably distinguishing between the
unconscious source of myths and the consciousness of that source. Presumably, he
is saying that ancient interpreters, like their modern, psychoanalytic counterparts,
recognized the unconscious source of myths. Otherwise the true meaning of myths
would have remained unknown.

"BIOS AND MYTHOS"

In his essay in the Festschrift for the Freudian anthropologist Géza Róheim
(Campbell 1951) Campbell first contrasts those who stress the differences among
myths--Malinowski and other functionalists--to those who, like Róheim, stress the
similarities. Functionalists, he argues, fail to see the difference between function,
where differences undeniably lie, and "homology," where similarities lie
(1951:330-336). How functionalists, who invariably maintain that myth serves the
same function in every society, stress only differences it is hard to see. Indeed, so
intent are functionalists on finding similarities that they typically look for the
functional equivalent of myth--for example, ideology--in societies that lack myth
itself. In subsequent works Campbell himself lists four functions that myth serves
everywhere.

It is no clearer what Campbell means by the homologies that unite myths than
by the functions that somehow divide them. Having in any case argued for
similarities in the form of homologies, he argues for independent invention rather
than diffusion as their cause. He does not deny that diffusion occurs. He merely
relegates it to a secondary cause. It can account for similarities within a "culture
sphere," where diffusion occurs, but not for similarities that cut across culture
spheres:

However, it is important not to lose sight of the fact that the
mythological archetypes (Bastian's Elementary Ideas) cut across the
boundaries of these culture spheres and are not confined to any one or
two, but are variously represented in all. For example, the idea of
survival after death seems to be about coterminous with the human
species; so also that of the sacred area (sanctuary), that of the

efficacy of ritual, of ceremonial decorations, sacrifice, and of magic,
that of supernal agencies, that of a transcendental yet ubiquitously
immanent sacred power (mana, wakonda, śakti, etc.), that of a
relationship between dream and the mythological realm, that of
initiation, that of the initiate (shaman, priest, seer, etc.), and so on,
for pages. (1951:333)[1]

By archetypes, which is Campbell's most common term for the similarities
among myths, he does not, like Jung, necessarily mean inherited rather than
acquired similarities. Here, as elsewhere,[2] he may well be using the term for the
products of similar experiences. As in *Hero*, so here: Campbell compares myths
with dreams and deems both the product of the unconscious (1951:335). But in
both works he neglects to explain the origin of the contents of that unconscious.

THE MASKS OF GOD

In *Hero* Campbell deals primarily with whole myths. Though he deals as well
with individual archetypes--for example, the hero, the call, and the mother goddess
--he subsumes them under the stories in which they appear. By contrast, in *Masks*,
as in the later *Mythic Image*, Campbell deals primarily with archetypes themselves.
He is interested less in the plots of myths than in the archetypal elements--the
characters and events--of which the plots are composed.

At the outset of *Masks: Primitive* Campbell attributes the similarities among
myths--the presence in them of the same archetypes--to independent invention
rather than diffusion. But independent invention must itself be explained. There are
two possible explanations: heredity, which is likely Campbell's explanation in
Hero, and experience. Where for Jung only inherited causes are archetypal, for
Campbell, who thus uses the term far more loosely, even acquired ones can be.

By archetypes Campbell, like Jung, means not just recurrent mythological
motifs but ones that stir emotion and propel behavior. But since by definition all
genuine mythological motifs do so, all of them are archetypal.

In *Masks* Campbell invokes the ethological studies of Niko Tinbergen and
Konrad Lorenz to explain archetypes. Archetypes, he proposes, are the releasers of
what, according to these ethologists, directly prompt emotions and actions in
animals: innate releasing mechanisms (IRM's).[3] Archetypes are the stimuli, or
triggers, that activate IRM's, which in turn are the stimuli, or triggers,[4] that activate
emotions and actions. Archetypes are to IRM's as IRM's are to emotions and
actions. Yet archetypes themselves need to be activated, and it is concrete symbols
that are the stimuli, or triggers, that activate them.

IRM's, believes Campbell, are found in humans as well as animals. The
difference between the IRM's of humans and those of animals is that human ones
respond to stimuli--archetypes--that are largely implanted by experience where
animal ones respond to stimuli that are largely innate. Human stimuli are largely
conditioned rather than unconditioned. Campbell cites the classic case of the innate
response of newborn chicks to the sight of a hawk:

Chicks with their eggshells still adhering to their tails dart for cover
when a hawk flies overhead, but not when the bird is a gull or duck,
heron or pigeon.... Here we have an extremely precise image--never
seen before, yet recognized with reference not merely to its form but
to its form in motion, and linked, furthermore, to an immediate,
unplanned, unlearned, and even unintended system of appropriate
action: flight, to cover. The image of the inherited enemy is already
sleeping in the nervous system, and along with it the well-proven
reaction. (1959:31)[5]

An actual hawk is a symbol. The category hawk is the archetype. The releaser
of the emotion of fear and the action of flight is the IRM. Though the archetype
needs a releaser--an actual hawk--to work, it itself is clearly innate. For the chick
experiences fear and scurries for cover before it has ever encountered any hawks.
    Campbell grants that some of the stimuli to which humans respond are innate.[6]
In fact, he even grants that some of the stimuli to which animals respond are
acquired.[7] His claim is that humans respond to far more acquired stimuli than do
animals:

But it must not be forgotten that the entire instinct structure of man
is much more open to learning and conditioning than that of animals,
so that when evaluating human behavior we have always a very much
stronger factor of individual experience to consider than when
measuring ... the innate releasing mechanisms (IRMs) of insect, fish,
bird--or even ape. (1959:37)

Echoing Róheim,[8] Campbell attributes this difference to the greater immaturity
of humans at birth: "It is by now a commonplace of biological thought to observe
that man ... is born at least a year too soon, completing in the sphere of society a
development that other species accomplish within the womb" (1959:38). Because
humans take longer to mature, they are more open to experience and therefore to
imprinting: "... whereas even the animals most helpless at birth mature very
quickly, the human infant is utterly helpless during the first dozen years of its
existence and ... is completely subject to the pressures and imprints of its local
society" (1959:36-37).[9]
    The experiences that, for Campbell, have imprinted the most powerful stimuli,
or archetypes, on humans are suffering, gravity, light and dark, male and female,
birth, breast feeding, excreting, Oedipus and Electra Complexes, puberty, and old
age (1959:ch. 2).[10] Some of these experiences are lifelong. Others occur only at
stages in life. Once imprinted, a stimulus, upon activation by subsequent
experience, activates an IRM, which in turn impels the corresponding emotion and
behavior. Without the archetype the subsequent experience would make much less
of an impact. The power of past experiences, imprinted in the form of an archetype,
accounts for its impact. Functioning as a symbol, subsequent experience activates

the archetype and thereby begins the process that ends in the manifestation of emotion and behavior.

In his emphasis on acquired rather than innate stimuli,[11] Campbell is Freudian rather than Jungian. Jung stresses innate stimuli, to which, as noted, he restricts the term archetypes. Neither Freud nor Jung has any notion of IRM's, which Campbell inserts between archetypes and the feelings and actions provoked.[12] For Jung, present experience activates the innate archetypes that in turn activate feelings and actions.[13] For Freud, present experience activates the equivalent of acquired archetypes, archetypes acquired through past experience. Where for Jung the experience of one's mother activates the innate archetype of the Great Mother, for Freud that experience activates an impression--the equivalent of an acquired archetype--made by one's prior experience of her.[14]

As intent as Campbell is at the outset of *Masks* to prove that the similarities in myths stem from similar experiences,[15] no sooner does he make his case (1959:part I) than he turns abruptly to differences in myths stemming from different experiences. Primitive hunters and planters have opposed kinds of experiences and therefore opposed kinds of myths. Moreover, those experiences have nothing to do with any of the universal experiences that Campbell presents in part one of *Masks: Primitive*. They are entirely economic. In subsequent volumes of *Masks* Campbell also stresses the differences in myths, but now he attributes them less to differing experiences of any kind than to differing metaphysical beliefs.

At the same time Campbell, in all but volume four of *Masks*, then proceeds to deny the very differences that he has enumerated. Once again, as at the start of volume one of *Masks*, all myths prove to be the same, though because the beliefs rather than any experiences underlying them are the same. Beliefs shape experience rather than, as in volume one of *Masks*, vice versa.

Despite Campbell's initial stress on experience as the source of the similarities in myths, he is continually preoccupied, from even volume one on, with diffusion rather than experience as the source. He is intent on arguing for the diffusion of myths within the West; within the East; from the East to the West; and above all from the "hieratic city state" of Sumer, the culmination of primitive planting, to all of the East.[16] So obsessed is he with diffusion as the cause of similarities that many reviewers understandably assume that he is contradicting his initial, experiential explanation.[17]

Perhaps there is no contradiction. Perhaps Campbell is attributing to diffusion similarities in symbols--for example, the pervasiveness of an Odysseus-like hero-- and is ascribing to experience similarities in archetypes--the pervasiveness of a hero per se. But the similarities he attributes to diffusion--notably, the concept of a hieratic city state--are so broad as to seem to be archetypes, not mere symbols.

In an essay (Campbell 1969:ch. 4) devoted to explaining the similarities between the archetypes of a single Sioux Indian myth and those of other myths worldwide, Campbell goes so far as to juxtapose diffusion and independent invention as equally plausible hypotheses:

Who will say by what miracle--whether of history or of psychology-- these two homologous images came into being, the one in India and the other in North America? It is, of course, possible that either one of the two paths of diffusion just described may have been followed. However, it is also possible that the two images were independently developed by some process of *convergence*, as an "effect," to use Frazer's words again, "of similar causes acting alike on the similar constitution of the human mind in different countries and under different skies": for in India, too, there was a meeting and joining of animal and plant cultures when the Aryans with their herds arrived in the Dravidian agricultural zone. Analogous processes may have been set in play--as in two separate alchemical retorts. (1969:104)

Here Campbell is clearly deeming diffusion and independent invention rival explanations, in which case diffusion, like independent invention, must be intended to account for archetypes themselves, not just for symbols.

THE MYTHIC IMAGE

In *The Mythic Image* Campbell, as in both *Hero* and "Bios and Mythos," compares myths with dreams and says that both come from the unconscious: "This argument is, briefly, that through dreams a door is opened to mythology, since myths are of the nature of dream, and that, as dreams arise from an inward world unknown to waking consciousness, so do myths ..." (1974:xi). Whether the contents of the unconscious are acquired or inherited Campbell once again fails to say. Taking the comparison between myths and dreams much farther than he does in either *Hero* or "Bios and Mythos," he contends that myths, like dreams, are composed less of plots than of images; have a logic of their own; and can only be experienced, not analyzed.

Yet in explaining the similarities among myths, Campbell, as inexplicably as in *Masks*, downplays the importance of independent invention, under which the unconscious falls, and focuses instead on diffusion.[18] At the same time it is unclear what portions of myth get diffused. Are mythic "images," the elements that get diffused, the archetypes composing myths or only the symbols expressing those archetypes? What Campbell means by archetypes is clear: sleep, dream, death, rebirth, child savior, virgin birth, world mountain, great goddess, cyclical time, axis mundi, primeval waters, serpent, sacrifice, awakening, and lotus. Whether "mythic images" are these archetypes themselves or only the symbols expressing them is the question.

Though Campbell himself does not explicitly deny the possibility, it is unlikely that concrete symbols expressing archetypes are what come from the unconscious. It is much more likely that archetypes themselves do. If the images are archetypes themselves, then Campbell is inconsistent: he is attributing archetypes both to diffusion, for it is the images that are diffused, and to the unconscious, for it is the archetypes that most likely stem from the unconscious. If, however, the images are the particular symbols expressing archetypes, then Campbell is consistent: he is attributing the archetypes to the unconscious, which is a form of independent invention, and their expression to diffusion. In that case he would be like Jung, though Jung downplays diffusion even when he grants the possibility of it.[19]

Though Campbell never says what his view is,[20] his prime example of diffusion--the recurrence of the number 432 and its multiples (1974:72-74)[21]--is so specific as almost certainly to be a symbol rather than an archetype.[22] Since, again, images are the entities diffused, they would therefore constitute symbols, not archetypes.

Whether it is symbols or archetypes that get diffused, it is from Mesopotamia that, for Campbell, high civilization spread to the rest of the world (1974:74). As in *Masks*, so here: Mesopotamia--for some reason Campbell no longer specifies Sumer--developed the notion of a hieratic city state, in which everyone had a fixed place that mirrored the place everything had in the cosmos. Only Mesopotamian science, claims Campbell, was capable of making the observations on which the number 432 rests (1974:74).

HISTORICAL ATLAS OF WORLD MYTHOLOGY

In the *Atlas*, as in both *Masks* and *The Mythic Image*, Campbell ascribes the similarities in myths to at once independent invention and diffusion. It is as likely here as in *The Mythic Image* that he is attributing similarities in symbols to diffusion and similarities in archetypes to independent invention. Hence one of the prime similarities he ascribes to diffusion, the widespread worship of the bear (1983:147-155), is far more likely the symbol of some archetype than an archetype itself.

Yet just as it is still not fully clear whether Campbell is attributing similar archetypes to independent invention or diffusion, so, as in all his other works save *Masks: Primitive*, it is not clear whether by independent invention he means experience or heredity. On the one hand he cites recurrent universal experiences: "For the phases of the moon were the same for Old Stone Age man as they are for us; so also were the processes of the womb" (1983:68). Here Campbell reintroduces the concept of IRM's (1983:47-49), though he concentrates on the imprint made by the experience of death alone[23] rather than by any of the other experiences he describes in part one of *Masks: Primitive*.

On the other hand, and in contrast to the stress in part one of *Masks: Primitive* on perennial human experiences, Campbell cites wholly primitive experiences that still stir moderns:

The animal envoys of the Unseen Power no longer serve, as in primeval times, to teach and to guide mankind. Bears, lions, elephants, ibexes, and gazelles are in cages in our zoos. Man is no longer the newcomer in a world of unexplored plains and forests, and our immediate neighbors are not wild beasts but other human beings .... Neither in body nor in mind do we inhabit the world of those hunting races of the Paleolithic millennia .... Memories of their animal envoys still must sleep, somehow, within us; for they wake a little and stir when we venture into [the] wilderness. They wake in terror to thunder. And again, they wake, with a sense of recognition, when we enter any one of those great painted caves. (1983:73)

Here Campbell echoes the early Jung, for whom subsequent mankind inherits the impact of the experiences of his forebears.

NOTES

[1] When, in later works, Campbell argues for diffusion, he uses the term "zone of diffusion" rather than "culture sphere": see, for example, Campbell 1959:387.

[2] See, for example, Campbell 1959:21-29.

[3] See Campbell 1959:21-131; 1973:44-47, 216-221; 1983:47-48. See also Niko Tinbergen, *The Study of Instinct* (Oxford: Clarendon, 1951), esp. ch. 2; Konrad Lorenz, *Behind the Mirror*, tr. Ronald Taylor (New York: Harcourt Brace Jovanovich, 1977), esp. chs. 4-6. For a brief summary of the concept of innate releasing mechanisms see John Alcock, *Animal Behavior*, third ed. (Sunderland, MA: Sinauer, 1984), 93-96.

[4] Besides "stimuli," Campbell calls archetypes "sign stimuli," "releasers," "images," "imprints," and "impressions."

[5] For other cases of innate stimuli in animals see Anthony Stevens, *Archetypes* (New York: Morrow, 1983), ch. 4.

[6] But see Campbell 1959:48, where he questions whether any human stimuli are innate.

[7] See, for example, the contrast Campbell draws between the acquired stimuli of ducks and the innate ones of chicks: see Campbell 1959:35. For other cases of acquired stimuli in animals see Stevens, 51.

[8] See ch. 10, pp. 112-116.

[9] See also Campbell 1973:44-45, 219-220.

[10] See also Campbell 1969:107-108, 110-111.

[11] IRM's that respond to only innate stimuli are called "closed," or stereotyped"; those that respond to acquired ones as well are called "open": see Campbell 1959:35-36.

[12] To be sure, Campbell, who is not fully clear, perhaps means that archetypes are the IRM's themselves. In his attempt to reduce Jung's irreducibly psychological archetypes to something physiological Stevens (passim, esp. 39) explicitly equates the two.

[13] To be sure, Jung initially believed that archetypes were acquired by prehistoric man in response to his experience. The continual experience of the power of the sun, for example, eventually imprinted on prehistoric man an archetype of it: see, for example, Jung, "The Structure of the Psyche," in his *The Structure and Dynamics of the Psyche*, The Collected Works, VIII, first ed. (New York: Pantheon, 1960), 139-158. Later, Jung came to believe that archetypes were innate in even prehistoric man, whose experience of the sun reflected rather than, as Jung had initially assumed, shaped the corresponding archetype. Where archetypes originated Jung now considered a metaphysical rather than empirical question and declined to say. Yet even early Jung assumed that archetypes, once implanted in prehistoric man, got transmitted to his descendants through heredity. Subsequent mankind thus inherited rather than acquired archetypes, though its experiences created new archetypes in turn.

[14] Freud scarcely denies that incestuous desires themselves are innate, but the Oedipus Complex involves one's experience of those desires, which includes the reaction of his parents. His encounter with them leaves an impression that constitutes, in Campbell's terms, an acquired stimulus. Only if the impression existed independently of the child's contact with his parents would the stimulus be innate.

[15] To be sure, myths are not the same as the archetypes imprinted on the mind by experience. They are the stories in which archetypes get expressed.

[16] See ch. 3, pp. 35-36.

[17] On the contradictions in Campbell's explanation see, for example, Morris E. Opler, review of *Masks: Primitive, Journal of American Folklore*, 75 (January-March 1962), 83; Ruth Fredericks, review of *Masks: Primitive, Bulletin of the Analytical Psychology Club of New York*, 21 (December 1959), 9. See also Alan W. Watts, review of *Masks: Oriental, Saturday Review*, 45 (June 2, 1962), 36: Watts contrasts Campbell's stress on diffusion in *Masks* to his stress on an inherited common unconscious in *Hero*.

[18] See esp. Campbell 1974:72, 74, 121, 292.

[19] See ch. 11, pp. 128-129.

[20] The fact that reviewers differ over Campbell's intentions shows how unclear he is. Joseph Henderson (*Quadrant* 8 [Summer 1975], 70) assumes that independent invention, by which he assumes an inherited unconscious, is supposed

to account for archetypes themselves and diffusion for only their symbolic expressions, which he calls "cultural forms." Conversely, John Gardner (*New York Times Book Review* [December 28, 1975], 15-16), William Doty (*Parabola*, 1 [Winter 1976], 101), William Kerrigan ("The Raw, The Cooked and the Half-Baked," *Virginia Quarterly Review*, 51 [Autumn 1975], 649-650), Ruth Hoffman (*Journal of Analytical Psychology*, 22 [July 1977], 280), and Richard J. Clifford (*Bulletin of the American Schools of Oriental Research* , No. 223 [October 1976], 76) all assume that for Campbell diffusion accounts for archetypes themselves, so that Campbell is replacing independent invention with diffusion. These reviewers simply ignore Campbell's attribution of myth to the unconscious, which is a brand of independent invention. Peter Green (*Washington Post Book World* [April 20, 1975], 4) says that Campbell simply alternates between diffusion and independent invention as the explanation of archetypes themselves.

[21] Campbell uses this same example repeatedly: see, for example, Campbell 1962:115-121, 129; 1964:459-460.

[22] In fact, Campbell himself (1974:72) appeals to the specificity of the number 432 to argue for diffusion over independent invention, which would constitute too great a coincidence.

[23] See Campbell 1983:25, 47, 52-56. See also Campbell 1973:20.

Chapter Ten

THE FUNCTION OF MYTH

THE HERO WITH A THOUSAND FACES

In *Hero* Campbell is concerned less with the function or even the origin of myth than with its meaning. He wants to show that the meaning of myth is both psychological and metaphysical. Insofar as he considers the function of myth, the function is to reveal to man the existence of a severed, deeper part of both himself and the cosmos:

> ... all the life-potentialities that we never managed to bring to adult realization, those other portions of ourself [sic], are there; for such golden seeds do not die. If only a portion of that lost totality could be dredged up into the light of day, we should experience a marvelous expansion of our powers, a vivid renewal of life. (1949:17)

Presumably, the hero's rediscovery of the severed reality provides a model for others to emulate.

Though Campbell focuses on the revelatory function of myth, if he focuses on any function, he may also be assuming an experiential function: myth may, for him, serve as a vehicle for actually encountering the severed reality, not just for learning of it. For myth, according to Campbell, does not just refer to archetypes but actually manifests them:

> For the symbols [i.e., archetypes?] of mythology are not manufactured; they cannot be ordered, invented, or permanently suppressed. They are spontaneous productions of the psyche, and each bears within it, undamaged, the germ power of its source. (1949:4)[1]

Insofar as the meaning of myth is either psychological or metaphysical, there seems to be no place for a social function. If myth serves to reconnect man with his

111

severed self, it operates solipsistically. If myth serves to reconnect man with the cosmos as a whole, it either trivializes or outright dissolves any distinction between man and anything else, including his fellow human beings.

Yet at least once in *Hero* Campbell does say that myth deals with society. Put negatively, social problems stem from psychological ones, from the failure to tend to the unconscious: "... every failure to cope with a life situation must be laid, in the end, to a restriction of consciousness. Wars and temper tantrums are the makeshifts of ignorance ..." (1949:121). Exactly how the rediscovery of a severed part of either man or the cosmos would abet one socially Campbell never says.

"BIOS AND MYTHOS"

In his essay in the Festschrift for Géza Róheim[2] Campbell deals entirely with the function, not the meaning, of myth. Here (1951:336ff.), as elsewhere,[3] Campbell cites Róheim's stress in *The Origin and Function of Culture*[4] on the premature state of man at birth. Man, for Róheim, is born less developed than any other animal, is therefore more helpless, and is therefore more dependent on his mother. Birth is traumatic exactly because it constitutes separation from the mother, unity with whom has heretofore shielded the child from the world into which he is now thrust:

> Three factors are responsible for neurosis, a biological, a phylogenetic and a psychological factor. The biological factor is the protracted helplessness and dependence of the human infant. The intrauterine period is relatively too short as compared to most animals; human beings are born in an unfinished state.... [I]t is only from the object (the mother) that the infant can obtain protection against the dangers of a strange world and a prolongation of the intrauterine period of life. This biological factor is the basis of the primary danger situations it creates, the desire to be beloved, a desire which human beings can never give up.[5]

On the one hand every child remains dependent on his mother from birth until adolescence. Together with his father, his mother feeds, clothes, and shelters him. On the other hand every child remains so traumatized by his initial separation from her that he spends all of his life trying to overcome it. He seeks not just to retain his mother's aid but, more, to restore his prenatal bond with her. He tries to overcome birth itself and return to the womb.

But Róheim distinguishes between a neurotic, childish means of restoring this bond and a normal, adult one. A neurotic tries to restore his tie to his mother herself. He thereby remains fixated at birth. A normal person manages to break free not of the yearning itself, which is never transcended, but of the infantile means of satisfying it: the mother herself. He finds substitutes onto whom to displace or sublimate his maternal attachment:

We have compared neurosis and the sublimations which constitute the
bulk of our civilization. In both cases we find the same defense
mechanisms evolved on the basis of the infantile situation but while
in neurosis the archaic objects are retained and the fate of the
impulse must therefore be a frustration of some kind, the
characteristic feature of a sublimation is that the impulse is carried
over to a substitute object.[6]

For Róheim, all of culture, which provides these substitutes, is a series of
edifices constructed to keep individuals from ever again facing the loneliness and
the terror of the separation experienced at birth:

> Civilization originates in delayed infancy and its function is security.
> It is a huge network of more or less successful attempts to protect
> mankind against the danger of object-loss, the colossal efforts made
> by a baby who is afraid of being left alone in the dark.[7]

Substitutes for the mother include both other persons--one's father, one's
spouse, all of society--and the external world--unity with the cosmos itself. Indeed,
Róheim interprets magic, totemism, and rituals generally as means of achieving
mystical oneness with the world.

In *The Origin and Function of Culture*, which is one of his later works,
Róheim deals only in passing with myth. He deals more fully with it not only in his
earlier, more nearly Freudian works, in which myth fulfills the Oedipal desire for
intercourse with one's mother, but also in other later ones, in which myth fulfills
the infantile desire for reunion with her.[8] The mythic hero is still someone who
dares to kill his father, and his father still threatens him with castration or death--
not, however, because the father wants his wife for himself, as Róheim earlier
believed, but because he wants his son to sever his infantile attachment to his
mother and grow up.[9]

Adopting Róheim's view, Campbell declares myth a second womb:

> Society, as a fostering organ is thus a kind of exterior "second
> womb," wherein the postnatal stages of man's long gestation--much
> longer than that of any other placental--are supported and defended....
> Rites, then, together with the mythologies that support them,
> constitute the second womb, the matrix of the postnatal gestation of
> the placental *Homo sapiens*.... Mythology is the womb of mankind's
> initiation to life and death. (1951:337, 339, 336)

How myth, which is not limited to hero myths, serves as a second womb
Campbell fails to say. Most likely, it explains the world and gives man a firm place
within it. Most likely, god takes the place of not, as for Freud in *The Future of an
Illusion*, a child's father but an infant's mother.

Even if Róheim distinguishes between normal and neurotic means of
preserving the prenatal bond, he, like Freud, still deems myth regressive. Where

for Freud myth expresses the childhood, Oedipal desire for intercourse with one's mother, for Róheim it expresses the even earlier, infantile desire for absorption in the mother. The mythmaker or believer wishes not to satisfy the id but to dissolve the ego.[10]

Though Campbell accepts Róheim's view of the substitutive function of culture, of which myth is a part, he also ventures beyond Róheim. For he envisions the possibility of breaking with not just the mother herself but even substitutes for her. He envisions the possibility of transcending the need for a substitute and so, most strikingly, the need for mythology itself. Indeed, he argues that the ultimate aim in the East, in contrast to the West, is exactly freedom from the mother and therefore from myth. Where the cowardly West seeks only substitutes for the mother in order to continue to cling to her, the brave East seeks independence of even them. Where the West seeks permanent return to the womb, the East seeks return as only a means to an end, which is rebirth in turn. Hence Campbell contrasts the Eastern desire to be born again to the Western desire to undo birth altogether:

> In India the objective is to be *born* from the womb of myth, not to remain in it, and the one who has attained to this "second birth" is truly the "twice born," freed from the pedagogical devices of society, the lures and threats of myth, the local *mores*, the usual hopes of benefits and rewards. He is truly "free" (*mukti*), "released while living" (*jivan mukti*) .... Within the Christian Church, however, there has been a historically successful tendency to anathematize the obvious implications of this idea, and the result has been a general obscuration of the fact that regeneration means going beyond, not remaining within, the confines of mythology. Whereas in the Orient ... everyone is expected, at least in his final incarnation, to leave the womb of myth, to pass through the sun-door and stand beyond the gods, in the West ... God remains the Father, and none can step beyond Him. This accounts, perhaps, for the great distinction between the manly piety of the Orient and the infantile of the recent Occident. In the lands of the truly "twice born" man is finally superior to the gods, whereas in the West even the saint is required to remain within the body of the Church and the "second birth" is read rather as being born [back] into the Church than born out of it. (1951:340)

In volumes two and three of *Masks*, however, Campbell reverses this interpretation of East and West: now the East preaches the sheer return to the womb and the West return from it. More accurately, the East, too, preaches return from it, but a return so devaluing the world to which one returns that, despite Campbell's claim to the contrary, there is barely any return at all. Ironically, Campbell in *Masks: Oriental* and *Occidental* continues to praise the East and damn the West, but now for reverse reasons.

In a theme that he argues throughout his writings Campbell says that modern, Western man is lost because he no longer has myth. Even though in "Bios and

Mythos" Campbell advocates a state beyond myth, he nevertheless considers myth necessary for achieving it: myth provides the necessary interim substitute for the mother. Like Róheim, Campbell labels neurotic anyone who lacks substitutes for the mother like it:

> Misbirth is possible from the mythological womb as well as from the physiological: there can be adhesions, malformations, arrestations, etc. We call them neuroses and psychoses. Hence we find today, after some five hundred years of the systematic dismemberment and rejection of the mythological organ of our species, all the sad young men, for whom life is a problem. Mythology leads the libido into ego-syntonic channels, whereas neurosis (to cite, once again, Róheim) "separates the individual from his fellows and connects him with his own infantile images." (1951:342-343)

Campbell would simply proceed to label neurotic anyone who did not abandon myth in turn.

In *Hero* myth functions to restore a primordial tie. In "Bios and Mythos" it functions to overcome one. At the outset of *Hero* (1949:6-7, 10-12) Campbell, citing Róheim's *Origin and Function of Culture*, does say that myth functions to surmount the infantile attachment to the mother:

> It has always been the prime function of mythology and rite to supply the symbols that carry the human spirit forward, in counteraction to those other constant human fantasies that tend to tie it back. In fact, it may well be that the very high incidence of neuroticism among ourselves follows from the decline among us of such effective spiritual aid. We remain fixated to the unexorcised images of our infancy, and hence disinclined to the necessary passages of our adulthood. (1949:11)

When Campbell cites Arnold van Gennep's work on rites of passage, he may be going so far as to say, as he does not do in even "Bios and Mythos," that myth, operating together with ritual, functions to surmount attachments to substitutes themselves for the mother:

> When we turn now, with this image in mind, to consider the numerous strange rituals that have been reported from the primitive tribes and great civilizations of the past, it becomes apparent that the purpose and actual effect of these was to conduct people across those difficult thresholds of transformation that demand a change in the patterns not only of conscious but also of unconscious life. The so-called rites of passage ... are distinguished by formal, and usually very severe, exercises of severance, whereby the mind is radically cut away from the attitudes, attachments, and life patterns of the stage being left behind. (1949:10)

Nevertheless, Campbell's overwhelming concern in *Hero* is not with detaching oneself from one's infantile state but with returning to it. Campbell's preoccupation is not, as in "Bios and Mythos," with the goal of the first half of life--separation from one's roots--but with the goal of the second half--reconnection with those roots. The attainment of the goal of the first half he simply takes for granted. Róheim himself would doubtless dismiss any return to one's roots in the second half of life as simply another vain attempt to return to the state prior to the first half, but Campbell does not. He distinguishes between an infantile attachment, which, contrary to Róheim, is surmountable, and an adult one, which is what his hero undertakes. Campbell's hero is heroic not because he manages to establish himself as an independent agent but because he dares to sacrifice his independence. In short, it is hard to see how Campbell's invocation of Róheim, who argues that even the nonneurotic fails to achieve the goal of the first half of life, is compatible with the rest of *Hero*, which argues for the attainability of the goal of the second half. But then since Campbell deems the goal of the second half of life the permanent return to the primordial state, the attainment of that goal would ironically put Campbell's hero in the same psychological state as Róheim's.

"Bios and Mythos" is a doubly incongruous piece: only here does Campbell restrict myth to the goal of the first half of life, and only here does he thereby seek to transcend myth. Everywhere else he deems myth indispensable, and indispensable for above all the goal of the second half of life--his regressive characterization of that goal aside. Where in "Bios and Mythos" Campbell dismisses myth as childish, if still useful, everywhere else he defends it against precisely this kind of charge--usually by arguing that myth seems childish only when wrongly taken literally as history or science. In associating myth in "Bios and Mythos" with childhood and in arguing for the need to venture beyond it, Campbell is at his most Freudian.

THE MASKS OF GOD

Because Campbell's analysis of myth in part one of *Masks: Primitive* is so different from his analysis in the rest of *Masks*, it makes more sense to consider the two separately.

In part one of *Masks: Primitive* the function of myth becomes much more positive than it is in "Bios and Mythos." First, myth ceases to be something to be superseded and becomes something to be used throughout life. The reason is that, second, myth ceases to serve merely as a substitute for the mother and becomes a means of breaking the attachment to even substitutes for her. Third, though Campbell still stresses human incompleteness at birth, the consequence shifts from human weakness--man's dependence on his mother--to human strength--man's malleability rather than fixity. Finally, myth ceases to deal merely with one's relationship with his family and becomes a means of forging relationships with society and the cosmos.

In part one of *Masks: Primitive* archetypes function to activate IRM's, which in turn activate emotions and actions. Myths, like dreams and rituals, provide the symbols that activate archetypes. A myth about Horus or Apollo, for example, might trigger the archetype of the sun, which is clearly akin to one of Campbell's universal archetypes: the alternation of light and dark. To experience the sun would be to experience it as more than a natural object. It would be to experience the sun magnified, perhaps deified: as something overpowering or alluring. The sun would stir feelings of either awe or security and behavior of either avoidance or exposure.

Natural as well as man-made symbols can serve to activate archetypes--for example, one's own mother as well as a female character in a myth or painting. But some archetypes may require an activation so strong that only a man-made symbol can stir it. As Campbell says of such "supernormal" symbols, or "sign stimuli"--a term that he uses for both the archetypes activated and, as here, the symbols that activate them:

> It was found, for instance, that the male of a certain butterfly known
> as the grayling (*Eumenis semele*), which assumes [i.e., reacts by
> assuming] the initiative in mating by pursuing a passing female in
> flight, generally prefers [i.e., reacts to] females of darker hue to
> those of lighter--and to such a degree that if a model of even darker
> hue than anything known in nature is presented [as a stimulus], the
> sexually motivated male will pursue it in preference even to the
> darkest female of the species.... Evidence will appear ... of the gods
> themselves [in myths] as [likewise] supernormal sign stimuli; ... that
> is to say, as an organization of supernormal sign stimuli playing on a
> set of IRMs never met [i.e., triggered] by nature [which lacked
> the stimuli needed to release them] and yet most properly nature's
> own, inasmuch as man is her son. (1959:43-44)[11]

Insofar as myths here serve to vent emotions and actions, their function is, roughly, Freudian--with the strong proviso that what is released need be neither repressed nor even unconscious. What is Freudian is the view of myth as a release.

But in part one of *Masks: Primitive* myth functions to do more than release emotions and actions. It also functions to interpret them. It interprets them in a variety of ways: psychologically, socially, and metaphysically. For example, the experience of the alternation of light and dark might, mythologically, become the dualism of soul and body or of good and evil--in oneself, society, or the cosmos. The experience of one's birth might become a metaphor for the experience of any transformation, or rebirth:

> In the imagery of mythology and religion this birth (or more often
> rebirth) theme is extremely prominent; in fact, every threshold
> passage--not only this from the darkness of the womb to the light of
> the sun, but also those from childhood to adult life and from the light
> of the world to whatever mystery of darkness may lie beyond the
> portal of death--is comparable to a birth and has been ritually

represented, practically everywhere, through an imagery of re-entry into the womb. (1959:61-62)

In part one of *Masks: Primitive* myth functions not only to trigger and to interpret emotions and actions but also to redirect them. By interpreting experiences, myths can create new ones. Though Campbell never quite explains how, myths can wean one from his mother and turn him to the external, adult world:

> Hence, although the rites certainly have a psychological function and
> must be interpreted in terms of the general psychology of the human
> species, each local system itself has a long history behind it of a
> particular sort of social experience and cannot be explained in general
> psychological terms. It has been closely adjusted to specific,
> geographically determined conditions of experience .... From culture to
> culture, the sign symbols presented in the rites of initiation differ
> considerably, and they have to be studied, consequently, from a
> historical as well as from a psychological point of view. It must be
> recognized that either view alone is an oversimplification.... On the
> psychological side, then, we may say that the boy is being carried
> across the difficult threshold, from the sphere of dependency on the
> mothers to that of participation in the nature of the fathers, not only
> by means of a decisive physical transformation of his own body (first,
> in the rite of circumcision ... and then, more cruelly, ... in the rite of
> subincision), but also by means of a series of intense psychological
> experiences, reawakening but at the same time reorganizing all the
> primary imprints and fantasies of the infantile unconscious. (1959:
> 90-91, 99)

In *Hero* initiation rites, which Campbell always deems mythological, likewise serve to replace the son's infantile attachment to his mother with an adult attachment to his father. But in *Hero* that goal becomes only a means to a mystical end: oneness with the father--and, indeed, somehow with the mother as well. Moreover, that oneness is likely not with one's actual parents but with the archetypes they merely symbolize.

In part one of *Masks: Primitive*, by contrast, initiation rites serve to replace the son's infantile attachment to his actual mother with a mature attachment to his actual father, and to do so as a means to a social end:

> So that, in sum, we may say that whereas the energies of the psyche
> in their primary context of infantile concerns are directed to the
> crude ends of individual pleasure and power, in the rituals of
> initiation they are reorganized and implicated in a system of social
> duty, with such effect that the individual henceforth can be safely
> trusted as an organ of the group. Pleasure, power, and duty: these are
> the systems of reference of all experience on the natural level of the

primitive societies. And when such societies are in form, the first two are subordinated to the last, which, in turn, is mythologically supported and ritually enforced. Ritual is mythology made alive, and its effect is to convert men into angels. (1959:117-118)[12]

In *Hero* myth initiates one into a strange, distant world, reachable only by leaving society. In part one of *Masks: Primitive* myth initiates one into his own society. Even if in *Hero* the proper hero returns to his society, he values it only because he finds the new world within it. In part one of *Masks: Primitive* the initiate learns to value his society itself.

For Freud, as for Campbell in "Bios and Mythos," myth serves to satisfy childhood desires and thereby to keep one stymied in childhood. For Campbell in part one of *Masks: Primitive*, as for Jung, myth serves to lead one past childhood, not to say infancy, to adulthood. Hence Campbell now criticizes Freudians for interpreting myths as regressive (1959:64-65, 91).

After part one of *Masks: Primitive* Campbell becomes concerned far more with the meaning of myth than with its function. Where in part one he almost presupposes the meaning and proceeds to consider its impact, after part one, as in *Hero*, he is principally devoted to the establishment of the meaning itself.

In *Masks*, which from now on will refer to everything but part one of volume one, myths are no longer limited to stories, as they are in *Hero*. Where in *Hero* myths are merely tied to religious beliefs, in *Masks* they seem to be religious beliefs themselves.[13] Even where myths are still stories, as they are in *Masks: Creative* above all, Campbell is interested in them as sheer beliefs. In *Hero* Campbell is certainly concerned with the beliefs expressed by myths, but he is also concerned with the way myths, as stories, express those beliefs. He is concerned with their plot. In *Masks* Campbell is concerned with only the beliefs themselves.

Because myths in *Masks* need not be stories, Campbell's view of myth here is far harder to apply to actual myths than his view in *Hero*. It is not coincidental that all of the applications of Campbell's view of myth are applications of the pattern in *Hero*.[14]

In *Masks* myth serves primarily to convey beliefs--but, in contrast to *Hero*, not necessarily beliefs heretofore unknown. Yet several times in *Masks*, and various places outside it, Campbell enumerates four functions of myth.[15] First, he says, myth functions to instill and maintain a sense of awe and mystery before the world. It does so either by putting god in the world or, in the wake of science, by making the natural world more complicated and therefore more elusive.

Second, myth functions to explain the world, which, says Campbell, religion used to do but now science tries to do. More precisely, myth functions to provide a symbolic image for explaining the world--for example, the image of the Great Chain of Being. As Campbell puts it elsewhere, "A mythology is a system of affect-symbols, signs evoking and directing psychic energies. It is more like an affective art work than like a scientific proposition."[16]

Third, myth functions to maintain the social order. It does so by giving divine justification to social practices and institutions--for example, to the Indian caste system. Fourth and most of all, myth functions to harmonize the individual with society, the cosmos, and himself. It serves to link him with everything both outside him and within.

Though Campbell presents these four functions several times in *Masks*, only at the end of *Masks: Creative* (1968:608-624) does he actually apply them to any myths. Since in most of *Masks* Campbell is only concerned with myths as expressions of metaphysical beliefs, what connection any but the second, explanatory function has with them is not clear. The mystical oneness that in much of *Masks* all myths purportedly preach would surely efface the very distinctions that the other functions presuppose: between man and the cosmos, man and society, and man and himself.

When, at the end of *Masks: Creative*, Campbell evaluates "creative" mythology by these four functions, he concludes that the tentativeness of scientific explanations precludes the fulfillment of the second function, which demands certainty.[17] Till now Campbell had scarcely associated creative mythology with science. Nowhere does he even say what in science is mythological. Perhaps he means the models and images used. In an interview he says that it is the disparateness of individual sciences rather than the tentativeness of science generally that makes it inadequate as a mythological explanation:

> We don't have the idea of micro-macrocosm--the little cosmos of
> man, the big cosmos of nature, and then the middle cosmos of society
> which shows the laws that govern them all. We don't have that same
> unity anymore. Physics and psychology really are not the same science
> anymore, although in their outermost reaches they're beginning to
> bump into the same mysteries. Still, you wouldn't take Einstein's
> formula as a guide to marriage. So the two spheres have broken apart
> and this is part of the problem of modern man.[18]

Yet elsewhere Campbell is considerably more optimistic. Rather than lamenting that science precludes mythology, he insists only that an effective modern mythology accord with science:

> To be effective, a mythology ... must be up-to-date scientifically,
> based on a concept of the universe that is current, accepted, and
> convincing. And in this respect, of course, it is immediately apparent
> that our own traditions are in deep trouble; for the leading claims of
> both the Old Testament and the New are founded in a cosmological
> image from the second millennium B.C., which was already out of date
> when the Bible was put together in the last centuries B.C. and first
> A.D.[19]

Still elsewhere Campbell says that the moon landing represents a potent contemporary mythic image:

> Let's look at the symbolic significance of the moon landing. Before
> Copernicus, man's images of the cosmos corresponded to what was

visible. The sun rose and set and the earth was obviously the center of the cosmos. Then Copernicus created a theory that removed earth from the center and placed it as one planet among many in the heavens. Although this theory has been intellectually convincing, it lacked the emotional impact of a cosmological image that was visible. You couldn't experience the new world view. Now, suddenly, through the eyes of the astronauts and the marvels of technology, we can stand on the moon and watch the earth rise over the lunar horizon.[20]

Indeed, a refrain throughout Campbell's writings is that man is continuously spinning myths, albeit private rather than public ones. Here the sole impediment to a modern mythology is modern man's obliviousness to the fact:

In the absence of an effective general mythology, each of us has his private, unrecognized, rudimentary, yet secretly potent pantheon of dream. The latest incarnation of Oedipus, the continued romance of Beauty and the Beast, stand this afternoon on the corner of Forty-second Street and Fifth Avenue, waiting for the traffic light to change. (1949:4)

In *Masks: Creative* Campbell argues that the individualism espoused by creative mythology renders impossible the fulfillment of the third, social function of myth as well as the second one (1968:621-623, 87). Elsewhere he says that relativism--the recognition of other customs and morals--makes it impossible to believe that the ways of any one society are divinely sanctioned by mythology.[21] In *Masks: Creative* Campbell may also be saying that the individualism inherent in creative mythology likewise precludes the fulfillment of the fourth, integrative function. Why, then, does Campbell introduce his four standard functions of myth, two or three of which the brand of mythology he himself touts above all fails to fulfill?

THE MYTHIC IMAGE

In *The Mythic Image* Campbell concentrates much less on the function of myth than on its origin and meaning. Myth functions in the same way that it does in *Hero*: both to reveal to man the existence of a deeper reality, whether psychological or metaphysical, and to enable him to experience that reality. As virtually so in *Hero*, so wholly here: Campbell ignores any social function of myth. Myth deals with man's relationship to either himself or the cosmos but not to society.

HISTORICAL ATLAS OF WORLD MYTHOLOGY

4 functions of myth

In the *Atlas* (1983:8-10) Campbell enumerates the same four functions of myth that he does in *Masks* and elsewhere. To the first function, that of instilling and maintaining a sense of awe and mystery before the world, Campbell now adds, as elsewhere, a sense of participation in it. Since Campbell now denies that myth serves to explain the world (1983:112), it is no longer clear what he means by the second, seemingly explanatory function. An explanation presented in the form of an image rather than a set of propositions would still seem to be an explanation. In *Masks* Campbell characterizes the fourth function as one of harmonizing the individual with society, the cosmos, and himself. Now, as elsewhere, he introduces a chronological aspect: guiding the individual through the stages of life.

In *Masks* Campbell discusses the four functions most fully in the volume on modern Western mythology, which he doubts is capable of fulfilling two or even three of these functions. In the *Atlas* he confines himself to primitive hunting mythology, which he is confident is capable of fulfilling all four functions.

NOTES

[1] Campbell puts the point far more straightforwardly elsewhere: "Within each person there is what Jung called a collective unconscious.... We penetrate to this level by getting in touch with dreams, fantasies, and traditional myths; by using active imagination" (interview with Sam Keen, in Keen, *Voices and Visions* [New York: Harper and Row, 1974], 73).

[2] See also Campbell, "Life's Delicate Child," review of Róheim, *The Origin and Function of Culture*, *Saturday Review of Literature*, 28 (October 13, 1945), 56, 58.

[3] See also Campbell 1949:6-12; 1959:45.

[4] Géza Róheim, *The Origin and Function of Culture*, Nervous and Mental Disease Monograph Series, no. 69 (New York: Journal of Nervous and Mental Disease, 1943). All citations are from the reprint: *The Origin and Function of Culture* (Garden City, NY: Doubleday Anchor, 1971).

[5] Róheim, 27.

[6] *Ibid.*, 122.

[7] *Ibid.*, 131.

[8] Representative of Róheim's earlier work are *Australian Totemism* (London: Allen and Unwin, 1925) and *The Riddle of the Sphinx*, tr. R. Money-Kyrle (London:

Hogarth, 1934), which stress the Oedipus Complex. Representative of his later work are *The Eternal Ones of the Dream* (New York: International Universities, 1945), and *Psychoanalysis and Anthropology* (New York: International Universities, 1950), which stress separation anxiety.

[9] See *ibid.*, 226.

[10] Though Freud originally downplayed the infantile relationship between mother and child in favor of the Oedipal one, he gradually came to recognize its importance. Still, he never accorded the fear of the loss of the mother the significance that he did the Oedipal fear of castration. Certainly he never gave it the importance that Róheim does. Róheim makes it not just the prime but virtually the sole human experience. He reinterprets the Oedipal conflict as the child's anger at the father for depriving him of unity, not sex, with the mother.

[11] See also Campbell 1959: 61.

[12] See also Campbell 1959: 60-61, 66, 90-91, 100.

[13] See the various objections to Campbell's loose usage in Northrop Frye, review of *Masks: Occidental, New York Herald Tribune Book Week*, 1 (March 22, 1964), 6; Joseph Fontenrose, review of *Masks: Creative, Western Humanities Review*, 23 (Spring 1969), 172; Fontenrose, review of *The Flight of the Wild Gander, Western Humanities Review*, 24 (Winter 1970), 87.

[14] See the bibliography for applications of Campbell's hero pattern. Campbell himself briefly applies the pattern to the Arabian Nights in his introduction to the *Arabian Nights*, ed. Campbell (New York: Viking, 1952), 14-17. Campbell also interprets the myth accompanying the Navaho ritual described by Jeff King as, in effect, an instance of the pattern he had not yet laid down: see Campbell 1943:51-84. Later he interprets the schizophrenic's "journey" in the same way: see Campbell 1973:ch. 10.

[15] On the four functions of myth see Campbell 1964:519-523; 1968:4-6, 608-624, 630; 1973:221-222, 1983:8-10; "Mythological Themes in Creative Literature and Art," in *Myths, Dreams, and Religion*, ed. Campbell (New York: Dutton, 1970), 140-144; interview with Keen, 72; interview with Lorraine Kisly, *Parabola*, 1 (Spring 1976), 72.

[16] Campbell, interview with Kisly, 78.

[17] See Campbell 1968:611-621; "Mythological Themes in Creative Literature and Art," 145-146.

[18] Campbell, interview with Kisly, 74.

[19] Campbell, "Mythological Themes in Creative Literature and Art," 144-145. See also Campbell 1973:4-7, 10.

[20] Campbell, interview with Keen, 84. See also Campbell 1973:ch. 11.

[21] See Campbell, "Mythological Themes in Creative Literature and Art," 145-146.

Chapter Eleven

CAMPBELL AS A JUNGIAN

Joseph Campbell is often labeled a Jungian.[1] He is certainly not a Jungian analyst and has undergone no Jungian analysis. If he is a Jungian, it is because he shares Jung's view of myth.

Campbell does cite Jung approvingly throughout his writings, far more often than he cites any other theorist of myth. Again and again, he favorably contrasts Jung's understanding of myth to that of not only nonpsychologists--for example, those who read myth literally--but, most conspicuously, Freud. He contrasts Jung's appreciation of the higher, adult meaning of myth to Freud's dismissive reduction of it to its childhood, sexual origins:

> Myths, according to Freud's view, are of the psychological order of dream.... Both, in his opinion, are symptomatic of repressions of infantile incest wishes .... Civilization itself, in fact, is a pathological surrogate for unconscious infantile disappointments. And thus Freud ... judged the worlds of myth, magic, and religion negatively, as errors to be refuted, surpassed, and supplanted finally by science. An altogether different approach is represented by Carl G. Jung, in whose view the imageries of mythology and religion serve positive, life-furthering ends.... [Myths] are telling us in picture language of powers of the psyche to be recognized and integrated in our lives .... Thus they have not been, and can never be, displaced by the findings of science, which relate rather to the outside world than to the depths that we enter in sleep. Through a dialogue conducted with these inward forces through our dreams and through a study of myths, we can learn to know and come to terms with the greater horizon of our own deeper and wiser, inward self. (1973:12-13)[2]

Freud
vs
Jung

More practically, Campbell has edited *The Portable Jung* and the six-volume selection from the *Eranos-Jahrbücher*, which, while not always Jungian, is always

125

Jungian in "spirit." Several volumes of his own works appear in the Bollingen Series, which is likewise Jungian in spirit. Indeed, two of Campbell's works constitute the first and the last entries in the Series. In addition, Campbell has edited various other Bollingen volumes. Furthermore, he has been both a fellow and a trustee of the Bollingen Foundation.[3]

But is Campbell therefore a Jungian? He never calls himself one. He praises Jung rather than defers to him. At most, he says that Jung has come closest to grasping the true meaning of myth. For example, having given his own interpretation of myths as the expression of universal archetypes, he says, "The psychologist who has best dealt with these [archetypes], best described and best interpreted them, is Carl G. Jung ..." (1973:216). If Campbell is truly a Jungian or even a kindred soul, he must surely share Jung's view of at least the origin and function of myth.

JUNG'S VIEW OF THE ORIGIN OF MYTH

The term "Jungian" often gets used loosely. Merely to be interested in myth is not to be Jungian. Innumerable non-Jungians are no less interested in it. Merely to deem myth important is, for the same reason, insufficient. Even to find similarities in myths is not enough. By definition all theorists of myth, as comparativists, do.

What *is* distinctively Jungian is above all the *explanation* of the similarities. There are two possible explanations: diffusion and independent invention. Diffusion means that myth originates in a single society and spreads elsewhere from it. Independent invention means that every society invents myth on its own.

Neither explanation assumes that the myths of any two societies are identical, only that they are similar enough to dictate a common cause. To be sure, diffusionists often argue that the similarities they find are too striking to be the product of independent invention.[4] But even they grant that the myths of no two societies are identical. Diffusionists and independent "inventionists" alike seek only to account for the similarities, not to deny any differences.

If the prime argument of diffusionists is that the similarities are too precise to have arisen independently, the prime argument of independent "inventionists" is that diffusion, even when granted, fails to explain either the origin of myth in the society from which it spreads or the acceptance of myth by the societies to which it spreads.[5]

To attribute the similarities in myths to independent invention rather than diffusion is not distinctively Jungian. Edward Tylor, James Frazer, and Freud, among others, do so as well. What *is* distinctively Jungian is the form independent invention takes. Here, too, there are two possibilities: experience and heredity. Independent invention as experience means that every society creates myth for itself. Independent invention as heredity means that every society inherits myth.

Independent invention as experience does not mean that every member of a society creates myth. Every member may well have the experiences that lead to its creation, but only a few members actually create it.

Independent invention as heredity means that every member of society not simply has the experiences that lead some members to create myth but, far more, has myth itself: every member is born with it. More accurately, every member is born with the elements that constitute the main content of myths: the similarities among myths that Jung calls archetypes. Here, too, only certain members of society create actual myths, but what they do is far more limited: they turn innately archetypal material into specific myths--for example, turning the archetype of the hero into the myth of Odysseus.

Tylor, Frazer, and Freud ascribe independent invention to experience. Jung is distinctive in ascribing it to heredity.

For Tylor,[6] everyone is born with a need to explain the world, but the explanations themselves are not innate. Everyone in primitive society, which alone has myth, doubtless experiences the same baffling phenomena that eventually lead to the creation of myths: the lifelessness of the body at death and the appearance of others in dreams. Every primitive likely seeks to explain these phenomena as well. But only a few postulate souls and then gods to explain them and finally spin myths to explain the actions of those gods. Because all primitives, for Tylor, experience the same perplexing phenomena, and because all primitive societies postulate gods to account for them, myths are bound to be similar. But each primitive society invents gods and myths on its own, in response to the similar experiences of its members.

For Frazer,[7] who is Campbell's grandest exemplar of independent invention through experience, everyone is born with a need not to explain the world but, more practically, to eat. No doubt everyone in society experiences hunger, but only the brightest members react by inventing first magic and then religion to explain how the world works and thereby how to secure food. There are no myths in the first, magical stage, which postulates mechanical, impersonal forces. Myth arises only in the next, religious stage, which postulates gods instead. On its own every society invents first magic and then religion. Every society invents its myths as part of its religion. As with Tylor, so with Frazer: similar causes are bound to yield similar effects, so that gods and therefore myths are bound to prove similar worldwide. Frazer puts the point in a line that Campbell repeatedly invokes as the clearest statement of independent invention through experience:

> ... the resemblance which may be traced in this respect between the religions of the East and West is no more than what we commonly, though incorrectly, call a fortuitous coincidence, the effect of similar causes acting alike on the similar constitution of the human mind in different countries and under different skies.[8]

For Freud,[9] everyone is born with an incestuous drive that surfaces at age three to five. Everyone experiences that drive for himself. From his ancestors he inherits only the drive itself, not their experience of it. Everyone in society also experiences frustration in trying to satisfy that drive. Some members of every society invent myth as an indirect, disguised, compensatory outlet for the blocked drive, which dare not be vented directly or overtly. Again, similar experiences are bound to give rise to, in this case, similar heroes and thereby similar myths. Hence Rank contends that all hero myths, if not all myths per se,[10] conform to the same pattern, one invented by each society on its own.

Like Tylor, Frazer, and Freud, Jung atttributes the similarities in myths to independent invention. But unlike them he attributes independent invention to heredity rather than experience. He claims that everyone is born not just with a need of some kind that the invention of myth fulfills but with the myths, or the contents of myths, themselves. More precisely, everyone is born with the contents of myths already elevated to the level of myth.

For Tylor, for example, the true content, or subject, of myth is the physical world. Mythmakers transform the impersonal forces of the physical world into gods and the behavior of those gods into stories. For Frazer, the same is true. For Freud, as represented by Rank, the true subject of myth is a child and his parents. Mythmakers transform the child into a hero, his parents into royalty or nobility, and their conflicts into stories.

For Jung, by contrast, the true subject of myth is the archetypes themselves of heroes and their adventures. The archetypes of the hero and his journey do not symbolize something else in turn. They are the symbolized. Because the archetypal level is the same as the mythic one, the mythic level is not invented but inherited. Everyone inherits the same archetypes, which together comprise what Jung calls the collective unconscious. In every society a few persons invent specific stories to express those archetypes, but mythmakers here are inventing only the manifestations of already mythic material. Odysseus, for example, gets either invented or appropriated to serve as a Greek expression of the hero archetype. Heroism itself is not invented, the way it is for Tylor, Frazer, and Freud. Only actual myths expressing it are.

For Tylor, Frazer, and Freud, experience, even if it is of innate needs, provides the impetus for the creation of myth. For Freud, for example, one's experience of his parents' reaction to his incestuous drives spurs the creation of myth. For Jung, by contrast, experience provides only an occasion for the expression of pre-existent archetypes. Archetypes shape experience rather than, as for Freud and the others, derive from it. The archetype of the Great Mother does not, as for Freud, result from the magnification of one's own mother but on the contrary expresses itself through her and thereby shapes one's experience of her.[11]

For Jung, as for Tylor, Frazer, and Freud, the differences among myths get transmitted by acculturation. But where for Tylor, Frazer, and Freud the similarities do not get transmitted at all--they are the product of the similar experiences of each society--for Jung they get transmitted by heredity. Again, the distinctiveness of Jung's explanation of the similarities in myth is not that he attributes them to independent invention rather than diffusion but that he attributes independent invention to heredity rather than experience.[12]

Independent "inventionists" of both varieties do allow for some borrowing among societies and therefore for some diffusion. They simply deny that diffusion can account for most of the similarities among myths--above all among societies too far removed from one another for any contact to have occurred. Thus Jung says:

Although tradition and transmission by migration certainly play a
part, there are ... very many cases that cannot be accounted for in this
way and drive us to the hypothesis of "autochthonous [i.e.,
independent] revival." These cases are so numerous that we are
obliged to assume the existence of a collective psychic substratum. I
have called this the *collective unconscious*.[13]

The additional standard argument against diffusion, also given by Jung, is that
even if diffusion can explain how contact takes place, it cannot explain how contact
takes hold and remains:

Now if the myth were nothing but an historical remnant [i.e., of
diffusion], one would have to ask why it has not long since vanished
into the great rubbish-heap of the past, and why it continues to make
its influence felt on the highest levels of civilization ....[14]

To maintain his distinction between archetypes, which are what get inherited,
and their symbolic expressions, which get created by every society, Jung could say
that independent invention accounts for the similarities in archetypes and diffusion
for any similarities in symbols. Exactly because symbols are ordinarily the creation
of each society, they usually differ from society to society--a Greek hero like
Odysseus differing from a Roman one like Aeneas. Jung could therefore attribute to
diffusion any similarities among specific heroes--for example, the obvious
influence of Homer's idea of heroism on Vergil. But in fact he attributes to similar
independent experiences similarities within classes of symbols--for example,
symbols of the cross--and attributes to diffusion only similarities in details--
symbols of specific kinds of crosses. Still, he never ascribes similarities to
heredity, which he reserves for archetypes themselves.

CAMPBELL'S VIEW OF THE ORIGIN OF MYTH

Is Campbell's explanation of the similarities in myths Jungian? In both *Hero*
and "Bios and Mythos" he attributes the similarities to the unconscious, which is a
form of independent invention. Indeed, in "Bios and Mythos" he relegates diffusion
to a mere secondary cause. But in neither work does he explain whether the
similarities, which he calls archetypes in any case, are, as for Jung, innate or, as for
Freud, implanted by experience. In *Hero* Campbell implies that the archetypes are
innate, but he never outright says so.
Campbell is less Jungian in *Masks* than in any other work except his Róheim
essay. On the one hand he is so intent on tracing cultural influences that he might
well seem to be attributing the similarities to diffusion rather than to independent
invention of either kind--experience or heredity. The possibility that he is attributing
to diffusion only similarities in symbols and is thereby allowing for independent
invention for archetypes does not seem to hold: the similarities he discusses are so
general as seemingly to constitute archetypes themselves rather than mere symbols.

On the other hand even if Campbell means to be attributing to diffusion symbols alone, the independent invention to which he would be attributing archetypes themselves is experience, not, as for Jung, heredity. To be sure, Campbell might here seem no different from early Jung, but for even early Jung the impact of the experiences of prehistoric man itself gets inherited. For Campbell, nothing does. Each generation creates archetypes anew out of its own experiences. It is presumably imagination which takes significant experiences and makes them mythical, or archetypal. Only the mechanisms for activating emotions and actions, the IRM's, are innate. Archetypes themselves, which activate the IRM's, are not.

How close to Jung Campbell comes in *The Mythic Image* depends on what Campbell means by "mythic images." The images, he stresses, are the product of diffusion rather than heredity or experience, but he never makes clear whether these images are archetypes themselves or only symbols expressing them. If, as seems more likely, they are archetypes, then Campbell is breaking fundamentally with Jung. If, however, the images are symbols, then Campbell is compatible with Jung, though, again, Jung attributes to diffusion only similarities in details. At the outset of *The Mythic Image* Campbell does say that myths come from the unconscious, but again he fails to say whether its contents are inherited or acquired.

If, in the *Atlas*, Campbell is attributing the presence in myths of the same archetypes to diffusion, then once again he is clearly far afield of Jung. But if he is attributing the presence of those archetypes not just to independent invention in general but to heredity in particular (1983:73), then he is obviously like Jung. Yet he would be closest to only early Jung since he would still be claiming that prehistoric man created, not inherited, his archetypes and simply passed them on to his progeny.

JUNG'S VIEW OF THE FUNCTION OF MYTH

To be Jungian is not merely to ascribe the origin of myths, or their contents, to heredity but also to ascribe to myths various functions. For Jung, myth serves, first, to reveal the existence of the unconscious:

> Myths are original revelations of the preconscious [i.e., collective] psyche, involuntary statements about unconscious psychic happenings .... Modern psychology treats the products of unconscious fantasy-activity as self-portraits of what is going on in the unconscious, or as statements of the unconscious psyche about itself.[15]

One who takes myth literally thinks that it is revealing the existence of something outside him--for example, god--but even unconsciously and certainly consciously it is in fact revealing the existence of his unconscious.

Myth serves, second, to guide one in dealing with the unconscious. The lives of the characters described in myth become models to emulate:

For instance, our ancestors have done so-and-so, and so shall you do.
Or such and such a hero has done so-and-so, and that is your model.
For instance, in the teachings of the Catholic Church, there are
several thousand saints. They serve as models, they have their
legends, and that is Christian mythology.[16]

Myth here assures one that others have had experiences like his.
    Myth serves, third, not just to tell one about the unconscious but actually to
open him up to it. Because one experiences the unconscious through only its
symbolic manifestations, the symbols in myth serve as a conduit for encountering
the unconscious. If on the one hand myth makes sense of any prior encounters, on
the other hand it itself constitutes an encounter.

CAMPBELL'S VIEW OF THE FUNCTION OF MYTH

    Though in *Hero* Campbell is concerned far less with the function than with the
meaning of myth, the functions he does implicitly attribute to myth are nearly
perfectly Jungian. Myth functions, first, to reveal the existence of a severed, deeper
reality, which Campbell, going beyond Jung, deems metaphysical as well as
psychological. Myth functions, second, as a vehicle for actually encountering that
reality. Since myth describes the hero's own rediscovery of that reality, his story
functions, third, as a model for others. But where for Jung myth fulfills these
functions even when its meaning remains unconscious, for Campbell myth works
only when "sages" reveal its meaning.
    In *The Mythic Image*, in which Campbell is also less concerned with the
function of myth than with its meaning, myth nevertheless serves the first two of
the three Jungian functions that it serves in *Hero*: to reveal the existence of a deeper
reality, whether psychological or metaphysical, and to enable man to experience it.
But Campbell here employs Kundalini yoga rather than Jungian psychology to
interpret that reality.
    In "Bios and Mythos" Campbell says what myth does but not how it does it.
What myth does is far from Jungian. Though it helps one grow up, it ceases with
the attainment of the goal of the first half of life. Going beyond the first half means
going beyond myth itself, which Jung would scarcely grant. The attachment that, in
the first half of life, myth helps overcome is, moreover, to one's mother herself,
not, as for Jung, to the mother archetype projected onto her. Whether in any case
myth helps break the attachment by, in Jungian fashion, providing a model
Campbell never says.
    Insofar as myths, in part one of volume one of *Masks*, serve to provide
symbols for expressing archetypes, Campbell's view of their function parallels
Jung's. But insofar as those symbols serve to activate archetypes, and in turn
emotions and actions, Campbell's view is more Freudian than Jungian. For Jung,
symbols in myths serve less to release archetypes than to reveal them. The payoff is
not relief but understanding. Even though Campbell does not deem archetypes
repressed or even unconscious, his stress on release puts him closer to Freud than

to Jung. Still, his stress on myth as interpreting the archetypes it activates fits Jung's view of myth, however non-Jungian his interpretation of those archetypes would be.

Elsewhere in *Masks*, together with the *Atlas*, Campbell lists four functions that all myths serve. The first two of those functions serve to link man to the cosmos. The third serves to link him to society. The fourth serves to link him to everything, including himself.

On the one hand Jung strongly opposes the rejection of the material world, including society, for the world of the unconscious. Ever seeking a balance between the one world and the other, Jung would applaud the third function, which, either intentionally or merely coincidentally, keeps man anchored to something material. Indeed, Jung would doubtless contrast this effect to the rejection of the material world typically sought by Campbell. On the other hand Jung cares more about connecting man to the unconscious than about connecting him to the material world, with which man has ordinarily not lost contact. Since only the fourth function deals with man himself, and since even it by no means necessarily deals with the unconscious, Jung would consider the functions as a whole askew to his concerns.

OTHER DIFFERENCES BETWEEN CAMPBELL AND JUNG

Even if Campbell and Jung agreed entirely on the origin and function of myth, they would remain far apart. Campbell, first of all, deems myth indispensable. No human being can survive without it. Undeniably, Jung values myth, but he does not consider it indispensable. Other phenomena--religion, art, dream, and the active imagination--can serve as well, even if at times Jung, like Campbell, uses the term myth to encompass all of them. The functions that myth serves may themselves be indispensable, but myth is not indispensable to serving them.

For Campbell, to have a myth is to accept it wholly. It is to identify oneself with the myth--for example, with the protagonist of a hero myth or the divinity of a creation myth. It is to live out the myth.

Jung is more critical. To have a myth is valuable but limited. A myth provides entrée to a side of oneself, but to only one side. Though a single myth can contain more than one archetype, no myth contains them all. An entire mythology--for example, that of Christianity or Hinduism--can deal with the whole of one's personality, but no one myth can. One should therefore have many myths. At the same time one should identify himself with none of them. To identify oneself with a myth is to lose touch with the rest of his personality, not least his ordinary, outward consciousness. Carried to an extreme, identification causes a breakdown rather than an enlargement of personality. Jung urges man to learn from myth without abandoning himself to it. More precisely, Jung urges man to discover the range of meanings of a whole mythology before committing himself to it. Properly understood, a complete mythology does accord a place to all sides of one's personality. One *should* live it out, but only upon recognizing its scope.

For Campbell, myth is not only necessary for the deepest human fulfillment but sufficient. One needs nothing else, including therapy. Indeed, therapy is only for those who lack myth.

Jung considers myth neither necessary nor sufficient for human fulfillment. Whenever myth is used, it must be used with therapy, which is an indispensable supplement, not alternative, to it.

Myth, for Campbell, contains all the wisdom man needs. All he need do is learn how to interpret it. He need never venture beyond it. Moreover, myth is easy to interpret. It invariably has a single meaning, even if wise men are needed to reveal that meaning.

Jung insists that man reflect on myth, not blindly accept it. If myth can guide one through life, it can also lead one astray. If myth can help one evaluate his life, one must also use his life to evaluate it. Furthermore, myth has no single meaning but an inexhaustible array of meanings.

For Campbell, to interpret a myth is to identify the archetypes in it. To interpret the *Odyssey*, for example, is to classify it as a hero myth, to show how it conforms to a heroic monomyth.

Jung considers the identification of archetypes the first rather than the last step in the interpretation of a myth. One must proceed to determine the meaning of those archetypes in the specific myth in which they appear and the meaning of that myth for the specific person who is stirred by it. The meaning of the myth for him is more than its general meaning for all mankind. One must analyze the person, not just the myth, to understand its significance for him. Hence the need for therapy. Hence Jung's distinction between archetypes, which are universal, and their symbols, which vary from case to case. Hence Jung's opposition to the adoption by the West of the specific myths of the East. Hence Jung's term for the ideal psychological state: "individua-tion." Many of Jung's disciples are no different from Campbell: they stop interpreting myth at the point of comparison, or "amplification."[17] But Jung himself does not.

For both Campbell and Jung, myth functions above all to link man to the unconscious, if also for Campbell to ultimate reality. But they differ over the final place of the unconscious. Though Campbell professes otherwise, he is in fact a mystic: he preaches absorption in the unconscious. Jung preaches balance: neither rejection of the unconscious nor surrender to it. What Campbell deems the psychological ideal Jung deems psychosis.

NOTES

[1] See, for example, Eric J. Sharpe: "The American scholar Joseph Campbell (b. 1907) has for many years been the major representative among students of comparative religion of the heritage of Jung. His industry has been remarkable, and he has in fact attempted a total Jungian interpretation of world mythology, particularly in the four volumes of *The Masks of God* ..." (*Comparative Religion* [New York: Scribner's, 1975], 212).

2 On the difference between Freud and Jung on myth see also Campbell 1959:31-32, 64-65, 91; 1969:49; interview with Sam Keen, in Keen, *Voices and Visions* (New York: Harper and Row, 1974), 75-76.

3 On Campbell's involvement in both the Series and the Foundation see William McGuire, *Bollingen* (Princeton, NJ: Princeton University, 1982), esp. xvii, 64-66, 121, 135, 139, 141-144, 158, 173-174, 177-179, 235, 277, 286, 291, 312.

4 See Campbell's own use of this argument: see ch. 9, p. 110n22.

5 See, for example, Otto Rank's appeal to the argument that diffusion can account for only the spread, not the origin, of myth: "Furthermore, the ultimate problem is not whence and how the material reached a certain people; the question is: Where did it come from to begin with? All these [diffusionist] theories would explain only the variability and distribution of the myths, but not their origin" ("The Myth of the Birth of the Hero," in *The Myth of the Birth of the Hero and Other Writings*, ed. Philip Freund [New York: Vintage, 1959], 5). By contrast, Jung argues from the reverse side: that diffusion cannot account for the *acceptance* of myth in other places. See below, p. 129.

6 See Edward B. Tylor, *Primitive Culture*, fifth ed. (New York: Harper Torchbooks, 1958), II (retitled *Religion in Primitive Culture*), esp. ch. 11.

7 See James G. Frazer, *The Golden Bough*, one-vol. abridgment (London: Macmillan, 1922), esp. chs. 3-4.

8 *Ibid.*, 448. Though Campbell cites this line repeatedly (for example, 1959:183, 1969:104, 1974:72, 1983:57), he gives the wrong page number. See also Frazer, 392: "It is no wonder that a phenomenon so important, so striking, and so universal should, by suggesting similar ideas, have given rise to similar rites in many lands."

9 See Sigmund Freud, *An Outline of Psycho-Analysis*, tr. James Strachey (New York: Norton, 1949), esp. ch. 7.

10 See Rank, 6-13.

11 See, for example, Jung on the origin of the archetype of the divine child: see Jung, *Symbols of Transformation*, The Collected Works, V, first ed. (New York: Pantheon, 1956), 222, 328, 330, 417-420; "The Psychology of the Child Archetype," in his *The Archetypes and the Collective Unconscious*, The Collected Works, IX, part 1, first ed. (New York: Pantheon, 1959), 161n21. To be sure, early Jung attributed archetypes to the imprinting of the experiences of prehistoric man, who then transmitted to his descendants the memory of those experiences.

Later Jung deemed archetypes innate in even prehistoric man. See ch. 9, p. 109n13.

[12] One might contend that independent invention through heredity is no invention at all. But independent invention does not require that every generation within a society invent myths anew. It requires only that one generation invent them rather than adopt those of another society. For Jung, every society experiences archetypes for itself and creates its own myths to express them.

[13] Jung, "The Psychology of the Child Archetype," 155. Ironically, Campbell himself (1983:57) cites this same passage as an example of independent invention rather than diffusion. Undeniably, Jung is saying that independent invention--for him, through heredity--is far more important than diffusion, but he is at least acknowledging that diffusion occurs. On Jung's view see Anthony Stevens, *Archetypes* (New York: Morrow, 1983), 40-41. For an example of the standard social scientific objection to Jung's minimizing of diffusion see Melville J. and Frances S. Herskovits, *Dahomean Narrative* (Evanston, IL: Northwestern University, 1958), 97-100, 102-103. Just as independent "inventionists" allow for some diffusion, so diffusionists allow for some independent invention. They credit it with explaining exactly the differences among myths--diffusion explaining the similarities. By contrast, independent "inventionists" claim to be able to account for the differences as well as the similarities among myths: the similarities are the product of the similarities among individual societies; the differences are the product of the differences. Independent "inventionists" attribute to diffusion the explanation of only minor similarities too detailed to have been independently created by individual societies.

[14] Jung, "On the Psychology of the Trickster-Figure," in his *The Archetypes and the Collective Unconscious*, 262.

[15] Jung, "The Psychology of the Child Archetype," 154-155.

[16] Jung, reply, in Richard I. Evans, *Jung on Elementary Psychology*, rev. ed. (New York: Dutton, 1976), 67.

[17]See, most grandly, Erich Neumann, *The Great Mother*, tr. Ralph Manheim, first ed. (New York: Pantheon, 1955).

CONCLUSION

On the one hand Campbell professes to be a defender of myth. His defense is twofold: that myth is both true and indispensable. Only when taken literally is myth false. When taken symbolically, which means psychologically and metaphysically, it is true:

> Traditionally, as I have already said, in the orthodoxies of popular faiths mythic beings and events are generally regarded and taught as facts .... When these stories are interpreted, though, not as reports of historic fact, but as merely imagined episodes projected onto history, ... the import becomes obvious; namely, that although false and to be rejected as accounts of physical history, such universally cherished figures of the mythic imagination must represent facts of the mind .... And whereas it must, of course, be the task of the historian, archaeologist, and prehistorian to show that the myths are as facts untrue ... it will be more and more, and with increasing urgency, the task of the psychologist and comparative mythologist not only to identify, analyze, and interpret the symbolized "facts of the mind," but also to evolve techniques for retaining these in health and, as the old traditions of the fading past dissolve, assist mankind to a knowledge and appreciation of our own inward, as well as the world's outward, orders of fact. (1973:10-11)

It would certainly be possible for myth to be true but useless. Myth might, for example, reveal the existence of something that was of interest to no one. Conversely, it would be possible for myth to be useful but false, even if its utility depended on the *belief* that it was true. For Edward Tylor, for example, myth functions superbly as an explanation of the world. The explanation it provides just happens to be false.

For Campbell, myth is both true and useful. On the one hand myth is not just to be believed but to be used--to "live by," as he titles one of his books. On the other hand myth is "usable" only because it is true. Admittedly, when Campbell says that myth functions to keep society intact, its efficacy depends on only the *belief* in its veracity: myth can doubtless work as effectively when members of

136

society believe it true as when it really is true. But when Campbell says, far more often, that myth functions to reveal a deeper reality, to enable man to experience that reality, to enable him to experience the world as awesome and mysterious, and to guide him through the stages of life, its efficacy depends on its veracity. To say that myth serves to reveal a deeper reality is surely to assume that that reality exists. Otherwise myth could not serve its function. Even to say that myth serves to guide man through life is surely to presuppose that myth is sufficiently in touch with reality to be able to guide him.

Most theorists of myth separate the utility of myth from its truth: myth need not be true in order to function. Most theorists separate as well the utility of myth in serving its function from the serving of the function itself: myth may be an effective means of serving its function, but it is rarely the sole means. As admirably as myth, for Tylor, serves to explain the world, science serves the same function at least as well.

Among theorists of myth, Campbell is distinctive, though not quite unique, not only because the utility of myth for him depends on its truth but also because myth alone serves its function. The profundity, abstractness, and scope of the functions he ascribes to myth make it hard to envision any alternative means of serving them. It is true that he defines myth so broadly that such obvious possible alternatives as ritual and religion get subsumed under it. But he still thereby deems myth unique.

Perhaps the clearest evidence of the indispensability of myth for Campbell is negative. Without myth, albeit myth misinterpreted literally, no individual and therefore no society can survive:

> For not only has it always been the way of multitudes to interpret their own symbols literally, but such literally read symbolic forms have always been ... the supports of their civilizations, the supports of their moral orders, their cohesion, vitality, and creative powers. With the loss of them there follows uncertainty, and with uncertainty, disequilibrium .... Today the same thing is happening to us. With our old mythologically founded taboos unsettled by our own modern sciences, there is everywhere in the civilized world a rapidly rising incidence of vice and crime, mental disorders, suicides and dope addictions, shattered homes, impudent children, violence, murder, and despair. These are facts; I am not inventing them. (1973: (8-9)

On the one hand, then, Campbell is the grandest of defenders of myth. On the other hand he is oddly not much interested in myth--as myth. He is much more interested in human nature, which he simply finds revealed in myths. He sees myths as a repository of the experiences and beliefs of mankind. He is far more concerned with the information myths contain than with myths themselves.

Campbell's true concern accounts for one conspicuous characteristic of his writings: that for all the attention he gives to myth he analyzes few myths. He cites hundreds of myths and extricates from them hundreds of archetypes, images, motifs, topics, themes, and values, but he analyzes few whole myths.

The reason is not that Campbell is a comparativist. Others as staunchly comparativist as he--Rank and Raglan, for example--concentrate on whole myths. The reason is, again, that he is interested less in analyzing myths than in using myths to analyze human nature. Where other comparativists, not to mention particularists, bring a specialized knowledge of one or more facets of human nature to bear on myth, Campbell does the reverse: he uses myth to elucidate human nature. Rather than using, say, sociology to explicate myth, he draws sociological conclusions from myth.

Obviously, Campbell does employ Freud and Jung to analyze at least hero myths. But even here his use is limited. He rarely uses them to explain either the origin or the function of myth. Because his interpretation of the meaning of myth is always at least as much metaphysical as psychological, even the meaning transcends whatever contributions they might make.

Campbell's indifference everywhere except *Hero* to the plot of myth evinces his indifference to myth as myth. To ask not just what myths reveal about the lives and convictions of human beings but how the plot expresses those revelations is necessarily to focus on the specifics of myths. Nearly everywhere but *Hero* Campbell isolates discrete elements within plots--the archetypal characters and events--and ignores the plots themselves. Even in *Hero* he analyzes no whole myths, only portions that express the archetypes that compose the plot. The fact that myths, for Campbell, can be rituals and creeds as well as stories underscores the minor role the plot plays.

Just as Campbell severs myths from their narrative context, so he severs them from their social one. He never asks: who created myths? Why did they do so? Who accepted myths? Why did they do so? Instead, he asks, What is the ultimate meaning, not of any particular myth but of all myths?

Though in volumes one and three of *Masks* Campbell does ascribe the differences between one group of myths and another to both economics--hunters and planters--and gender--patriarchy and matriarchy--he never utilizes any information about either economics or gender to understand these myths. Rather, he infers economic and sexual conclusions from the myths themselves. Moreover, the beliefs he deciphers are so abstract and sublime as to soar far above anything economic or sexual.

Certainly Campbell does not ignore the question of the origin and function of myth. Indeed, his concern with especially the origin makes him far bolder than most other contemporary theorists, who usually confine themselves to the function and meaning. But Campbell's most common answer to the question is still ethereal: myth originates and functions to reveal ultimate reality and to enable man to experience it. Who invents it and who uses it he never says. Even when, in part one of *Masks: Primitive*, he discusses at length the concrete, physical experiences that give rise to myths, the meaning of those experiences waxes so metaphysical as to transcend their source by far: the origin turns out to have no consequence for the meaning. Tying archetypes to the technicalities of IRM's seems almost incongruous because the meaning of the emotions and actions activated by IRM's and in turn by archetypes is so much more grandiose than the cause.

When, in *Masks* and elsewhere, Campbell presents four functions of myth, the same disparity surfaces between the concreteness of most of the functions and the abstractness of the meaning. Insofar as the uniform meaning of myth remains the oneness of all things, the very distinctions assumed by all four functions get effaced: is it not trivial, if not illusory, to seek to harmonize man with the cosmos, man with society, and man with himself when all of these entities are, according to the meaning, really one?

Furthermore, Campbell never explains how any of his functions actually operate. It is one thing to say *that* myth serves a function. It is another to say *how* myth serves it. Exactly how does myth serve to instill and maintain awe before the cosmos or to guide one through the stages of life? Where many other theorists try to work out the process, Campbell ignores it, for, again, he is not concerned with myths themselves.

None of these criticisms of Campbell follows from his comparativism. Rank's analysis of hero myths is no less comparative than Campbell's, but it is infinitely more precise, concrete, and complete. Rank seeks to explain what kind of person, under what circumstances, is likely to create or to adopt a myth. He seeks to explain both how and why myth originates and functions. Furthermore, he tries to connect the meaning of myth to the plot: he provides a set of rules--for example, the devices of projection and displacement--for translating the literal story into a psychological drama. Outside of *Hero* Campbell offers nothing of the kind.

Even Jung's analysis of myth, which often gets faulted on the same grounds as Campbell's, is far more detailed and down-to-earth. As argued in the previous chapter, Jung's analysis begins where Campbell's ends: with the identification of archetypes. Where for Jung that identification provides only a sketch of the meaning and function of myth, for Campbell it provides nearly the whole of both.

Because Campbell analyzes few myths, his views seem far more dogmatic than those of other, equally resolute theorists. An attempted analysis of actual myths would constitute one fair test of his claim that the meaning, not to say the origin and function, of all myths is universal rather than particular, symbolic rather than literal, nonhistorical rather than historical, and psychological rather than social. Instead, Campbell takes his claims for granted and, on the basis of them, extracts the experiences and beliefs of mankind from myths.

If on the one hand Campbell preaches that all things, including seemingly opposed ones, are really one, on the other hand he himself stresses various oppositions that seem artificial. Romantically pitting individual faith against institutionalized religion, he ignores the views of Max Weber and innumerable others that "institutionalization" is both a necessary and an inevitable process in the development of any religion. Similarly pitting the modern, Western individual against society itself, he ignores the views of Emile Durkheim and others that even individualism is the product of society.

A different kind of opposition is Campbell's distinction between experience and interpretation. In above all *The Mythic Image* and the *Atlas* he argues that mythic experience is the same worldwide and that subsequent interpretations by individual societies impose differences. Campbell's assumed distinction between

> An individual's faith does not develop
> & remain impossible & credulous.

experience and interpretation has been challenged again and again in psychology, philosophy, and other fields.

There are other criticisms that can be lodged against Campbell. He repeatedly contradicts himself on the central issues: why myths are the same, whether myths are the same, and what their message is. But these criticisms pale beside the prime one: that Campbell spends too much time reveling in myth and not enough time analyzing it.

BIBLIOGRAPHY

(1) BY CAMPBELL

(a) BOOKS

A Skeleton Key to Finnegans Wake. With Henry Morton Robinson. New York:
Harcourt, Brace, and World, 1944. Paperback: New York: Viking Compass
Books, 1961.

Edited:
The Works of Heinrich R. Zimmer:
Myths and Symbols in Indian Art and Civilization. Bollingen Series VI. New York:
Pantheon Books, 1946. Paperback: New York: Harper Torchbooks, 1962. No
second ed.
The King and the Corpse: Tales of the Soul's Conquest of Evil. Bollingen Series
XI. New York: Pantheon Books, 1948. Second ed.: New York: Pantheon
Books, 1956. Paperback: New York: Meridian Books, 1960.
Philosophies of India. Bollingen Series XXVI. New York: Pantheon Books, 1951.
Paperback: New York: Meridian Books, 1956. No second ed.
The Art of Indian Asia: Its Mythology and Transformations. Completed by
Campbell. 2 vols. Bollingen Series XXXIX. New York: Pantheon Books,
1955. Second ed.: New York: Pantheon Books, 1960.

The Hero with a Thousand Faces. Bollingen Series XVII. New York: Pantheon
Books, 1949. Paperback: New York: Meridian Books, 1956. Second ed.:
Princeton, NJ: Princeton University Press, 1968. Paperback of second ed.:
Princeton, NJ: Princeton University Press, 1972.

Edited:
Myth and Man Series:
Carl Kerényi. *The Gods of the Greeks*. London and New York: Thames and
Hudson, 1951.

Maya Deren. *Divine Horsemen: The Living Gods of Haiti*. London and New York: Thames and Hudson, 1953.

Alan W. Watts. *Myth and Ritual in Christianity*. London and New York: Thames and Hudson, 1954.

Edited:
The Portable Arabian Nights. Viking Portable Library. New York: Viking Press, 1952.

Edited:
Papers from the Eranos Yearbooks, trs. Ralph Manheim and R. F. C. Hull. Bollingen Series XXX:
Vol. I: *Spirit and Nature*. New York: Pantheon Books, 1954. Paperback: Princeton, NJ: Princeton University Press, 1982.
Vol. II: *The Mysteries*. New York: Pantheon Books, 1955. Paperback: Princeton, NJ: Princeton University Press, 1979.
Vol. III: *Man and Time*. New York: Pantheon Books, 1957. Paperback: Princeton, NJ: Princeton University Press, 1983.
Vol. IV: *Spiritual Disciplines*. New York: Pantheon Books, 1960. Paperback: Princeton, NJ: Princeton University Press, 1985.
Vol. V: *Man and Transformation*. New York: Pantheon Books, 1964. Paperback: Princeton, NJ: Princeton University Press, 1981.
Vol. VI: *The Mystic Vision*. Princeton, NJ: Princeton University Press, 1968. Paperback: Princeton, NJ: Princeton University, 1983.

The Masks of God:
Vol. I: *Primitive Mythology*. New York: Viking Press, 1959. Paperback: New York: Viking Compass Books, 1970. Paperback reprint: New York: Penguin Books, 1976.
Vol. II: *Oriental Mythology*. New York: Viking Press, 1962. Paperback: New York: Viking Compass Books, 1970. Paperback reprint: New York: Penguin Books, 1976.
Vol. III: *Occidental Mythology*. New York: Viking Press, 1964. Paperback: New York: Viking Compass Books, 1970. Paperback reprint: NewYork: Penguin Books, 1976.
Vol. IV: *Creative Mythology*. New York: Viking Press, 1968. Paperback: Viking Compass Books, 1970. Paperback reprint: New York: Penguin Books, 1976.

The Flight of the Wild Gander: Explorations in the Mythological Dimension. New York: Viking Press, 1969. Paperback: Chicago: Regnery Gateway Editions, 1972.

Edited:
Myths, Dreams, and Religion. New York: Dutton, 1970.

Edited:

The Portable Jung, tr. R. F. C. Hull. Viking Portable Library. New York: Viking Press, 1971.

Myths to Live By. New York: Viking Press, 1972. Paperback: New York: Bantam Books, 1973.

The Mythic Image. Assisted by M. J. Abadie. Bollingen Series C. Princeton, NJ: Princeton University Press, 1974. Paperback: Princeton, NJ: Princeton University Press, 1983.

Historical Atlas of World Mythology: Vol. I: *The Way of the Animal Powers*. Alfred van der Marck Editions. San Francisco: Harper and Row, 1983.

    (b) ESSAYS, REVIEWS, ETC.:

"Commentary" to *Where the Two Came to Their Father: A Navaho War Ceremonial*, given by Jeff King, text and paintings recorded by Maud Oakes, Bollingen Series I (New York: Pantheon Books, 1943), 51-84. Second ed. (with altered order): Princeton, NJ: Princeton University Press, 1969. Pp. 3-4, 7-8, 31-49.

"Folkloristic Commentary" to *Grimm's Fairy Tales*, ed. Josef Scharl, tr. Margaret Hunt, rev. James Stern (New York: Pantheon Books, 1944), 833-864. Reprinted in Campbell, *The Flight of the Wild Gander*, ch. 1.

"Life's Delicate Child," review of Géza Róheim, *The Origin and Function of Culture*, *Saturday Review of Literature*, 28 (October 13, 1945), 56, 58.

"Finnegan the Wake," *Chimera*, 4 (Spring 1946), 63-80. Reprinted in *James Joyce: Two Decades of Criticism*, ed. Seon Givens (New York: Vanguard Press, 1948), 368-389.

"Bios and Mythos: Prolegomena to a Science of Mythology," in *Psychoanalysis and Culture: Essays in Honor of Géza Róheim*, eds. George B. Wilbur and Warner Muensterberger (New York: International Universities Press, 1951), 329-343. Reprinted, minus subtitle, in Campbell, *The Flight of the Wild Gander*, ch. 2. Reprinted, in slightly abridged form, in *Myth and Literature: Contemporary Theory and Practice*, ed. John B. Vickery (Lincoln: University of Nebraska Press, 1966), 15-23. Reprinted in paperback reprint of *Myth and Literature* (Lincoln: University of Nebraska Press Bison Books, 1969), 15-23.

Review of C. G. Jung and C. Kerényi, *Essays on a Science of Mythology, Review of Religion*, 16 (March 1952), 169-173.

"Editor's Introduction" to *The Portable Arabian Nights*, ed. Campbell, Viking Portable Library (New York: Viking Press, 1952), 1-35.

"Heinrich Zimmer (1890-1943)," *Partisan Review*, 20 (July 1953), 444-451.

"The Symbol without Meaning," *Eranos-Jahrbücher*, 26 (1957), 415-476. Reprinted in partially revised form in Campbell, *The Flight of the Wild Gander*, ch. 5.

"Hinduism," in *Basic Beliefs: The Religious Philosophies of Mankind*, ed.
Johnson E. Fairchild (New York: Sheridan House, 1959), 54-72.

"The Historical Development of Mythology," *Daedalus*, 88 (Spring 1959), 232-
254. Reprinted in *Myth and Mythmaking*, ed. Henry A. Murray (New York:
George Braziller, 1960), ch. 1. Reprinted in paperback reprint of *Myth and
Mythmaking* (Boston: Beacon Press, 1968), ch. 1. Parts III and IV are
equivalent to the "Introduction" to *The Masks of God: Primitive Mythology*,
21-29; parts I and II are largely a summary of *The Masks of God: Oriental
Mythology* and *Occidental Mythology*.

"Renewal Myths and Rites of the Primitive Hunters and Planters," *Eranos-
Jahrbücher*, 28 (1959), 407-458. Reprinted in revised form as "Mythogenesis"
in Campbell, *The Flight of the Wild Gander*, ch. 4.

"Primitive Man as Metaphysician," in *Culture in History: Essays in Honor of Paul
Radin*, ed. Stanley Diamond (New York: Columbia University Press, 1960),
380-392. Reprinted in *Primitive Views of the World*, ed. Stanley Diamond
(New York: Columbia University Press, 1964), 20-32. Reprinted in Campbell,
The Flight of the Wild Gander, ch. 3.

"Oriental Philosophy and Occidental Psychoanalysis," in *Proceedings of the IXth
International Congress for the History of Religions*, Tokyo and Kyoto, August
27-September 9, 1958 (Tokyo: Maruzen, 1960), 492-496.

"Introduction" to Helen Diner, *Mothers and Amazons: The First Feminine History
of Culture*, ed. and tr. John Philip Lundin (New York: Julian Press, 1965), v-
x.

"Introduction" to *Myth, Religion, and Mother Right: Selected Writings of J. J.
Bachofen*, tr. Ralph Manheim, preface by George Boas, Bollingen Series
LXXXIV (Princeton, NJ: Princeton University Press, 1967), xxv-lvii.

"The Secularization of the Sacred," in *The Religious Situation*, vol.1 (1968), ed.
Donald R. Cutler (Boston: Beacon Press, 1968), ch. 17. Reprinted in
Campbell, *The Flight of the Wild Gander*, ch. 6.

"Mythological Themes in Creative Literature and Art," in *Myths, Dreams, and
Religion*, ed. Campbell (New York: Dutton, 1970), 138-175.

"Contransmagnificandjewbangtantiality," *Studies in the Literary Imagination*, 3
(October 1970), 3-18.

"Editor's Introduction" to *The Portable Jung*, ed. Campbell, tr. R. F. C. Hull,
Viking Portable Library (New York: Viking Press, 1971), vii-xxxii.

"On Mythic Shapes of Things to Come--Circular and Linear," *Horizon*, 16
(Summer 1974), 35-37.

"Seven Levels of Consciousness," *Psychology Today*, 9 (December 1975), 77-78.

"Erotic Irony and Mythic Forms in the Art of Thomas Mann," *Boston University
Journal*, 24 (1976), 10-27.

"Myths from West to East," in Alexander Eliot, *Myths*, with contributions by
Mircea Eliade and Campbell (New York: McGraw-Hill Book Company,
1976), 30-57.

"Foreword" to Rato Khyongla Nawang Losang, *My Life and Lives: The Story of a
Tibetan Incarnation* (New York: Dutton, 1977), vi-viii.

"The Occult in Myth and Literature," in *Literature and the Occult: Essays in Comparative Literature*, ed. Luanne Frank, UTA Publications in Literature (Arlington: University of Texas at Arlington, 1977), 3-18.

"Introduction" to *Bulfinch's Mythology: The Greek and Roman Fables Illustrated*, compiled by Bryan Holme (New York: Viking Press, 1979), 6-9.

"Foreword" and "Symbolism of the Marseilles Deck," in Campbell and Richard Roberts, *Tarot Revelations* (San Francisco: Alchemy Books, 1979), 3-7 and 9-25. Second ed.: San Anselmo, CA: Vernal Equinox Books, 1982. Pp. 3-7 and 9-25.

"The Interpretation of Symbolic Forms," in *The Binding of Prometheus: Perspectives on Myth and the Literary Process*, Collected Papers of the Bucknell University Program on Myth and Literature and the Bucknell-Susquehanna Colloquium on Myth in Literature, March 21-22,1974, eds. Marjorie W. McCune, Tucker Orbison, and Philip M. Withim (Lewisburg, PA: Bucknell University Press, 1980), 35-59.

"Joseph Campbell on the Great Goddess," *Parabola*, 5 (November 1980), 74-85.

"Masks of Oriental Gods: Symbolism of Kundalini Yoga," in *Literature of Belief: Sacred Scripture and Religious Experience*, ed. Neal E. Lambert, Religious Studies Monograph Series, vol. 5 (Salt Lake City, UT: Brigham Young University Press, 1981), ch. 6. Is largely reprinted from Campbell, *The Mythic Image*, ch. 4.

"Indian Reflections in the Castle of the Grail," in *The Celtic Consciousness*, ed. Robert O'Driscoll (New York: George Braziller, 1982), 3-30.

"Foreword" to Heinrich Zimmer, *Artistic Form and Yoga in the Sacred Images of India*, trs. and eds. Gerald Chapple and James B. Lawson in collaboration with J. Michael McKnight (Princeton, NJ: Princeton University Press, 1984), xv-xvi.

" 'Our Mythology Has Been Wiped Out' By Rapid Change," *U. S. News and World Report,* 96 (April 16, 1984), 72.

(c) INTERVIEWS

Abrams, Garry. "World Mythology in Modern Vogue." *Los Angeles Times,* 103 (January 13, 1984), Section V, 2, 26.

Auchincloss, Douglas. "On Waking Up: An Interview with Joseph Campbell." *Parabola*, 7 (Winter 1982), 79-84.

Barbato, Joseph. "Reconstructing a 'Life History' of the World's Myths." *Chronicle of Higher Education*, 28 (March 21, 1984), 5-7.

Bruckner, D. J. "Joseph Campbell: 70 Years of Making Connections." *New York Times Book Review* (December 18, 1983), 25-27.

Goodrich, Chris. "Joseph Campbell." *Publishers Weekly*, 228 (August 23, 1985), 74-75.

Keen, Sam. "Man and Myth: A Conversation with Joseph Campbell." *Psychology Today*, 5 (July 1971), 35-39, 86-95. Reprinted in Keen, *Voices and Visions* (New York: Harper and Row, 1974), 67-86.

Kennedy, Eugene. "Earthrise: The Dawning of a New Spiritual Awareness." *New York Times Magazine* (April 15, 1979), 14-15, 51-56.

Kisly, Lorraine. "Living Myths: A Conversation with Joseph Campbell." *Parabola*, 1 (Spring 1976), 70-81.

McKnight, Michael. "Elders and Guides: A Conversation with Joseph Campbell (On H. R. Zimmer)." *Parabola*, 5 (February 1980), 57-65.

Newlove, Donald. "The Professor with a Thousand Faces." *Esquire*, 88 (September 1977), 99-103, 132-136.

(2) ABOUT CAMPBELL

(a) REVIEWS

Reviews of *Where the Two Came to Their Father*:

Sergeant, Elizabeth S. *Saturday Review of Literature*, 27 (April 1, 1944), 17.

Reviews of *The Hero with a Thousand Faces*:

Chase, Richard. *Nation*, 169 (July 2, 1949), 17-18.

Davidson, H. R. Ellis. *Folklore*, 80 (Summer 1969), 156-157.

Deutsch, Babette. *New York Herald Tribune Weekly Book Review*, 25 (July 24, 1949), 7.

Flenniken, Margaret A. *Bulletin of the Analytical Psychology Club of New York*, 11 (May 1949), 5-7.

Hartley, Margaret L. *Southwest Review*, 35 (Winter 1950), xiv, 71.

Hyman, Stanley Edgar. "Myth, Ritual, and Nonsense." *Kenyon Review*, 11 (Summer 1949), 455-475. On Campbell: 455-456, 470-475.

Luomala, Katharine. *Journal of American Folklore*, 63 (January-March 1950), 121.

Parrinder, Geoffrey. *Expository Times*, 80 (July 1969), 305-306.

Radin, Max. *New York Times Book Review* (June 26, 1949), 23.

Reinhold, H. A. *Commonweal*, 50 (July 8, 1949), 321-324.

Troy, William. *Partisan Review*, 16 (September 1949), 952-955.

Reviews of *The Masks of God*:

Abrahams, Roger. *Midwest Folklore*, 10 (Fall 1960), 152-154.

Aldwinckle, R. F. *Canadian Journal of Theology*, 11 (October 1965), 291-292.

Anonymous. *Times Literary Supplement,* No. 3052, 59 (August 26, 1960), 548.

_____. *Times Literary Supplement*, No. 3216, 62 (October 18, 1963), 832.

Arnold, Bruce. "The Celtic Enigma." *Dublin Magazine* (Autumn/Winter 1968), 85-89. On Campbell: 85, 87.

Burridge, Kenelm. *Blackfriars*, 42 (June 1961), 282-283.

Carter, Charles. *Social Science*, 40 (April 1965), 120-121.

Crehan, Joseph. *Theological Studies*, 30 (March 1969), 156-157.

Dunn, Stephen P. *American Anthropologist*, 62 (December 1960), 1115-1117.

_____. *American Anthropologist*, 67 (February 1965), 140-141.

Fredericks, Ruth. *Bulletin of the Analytical Psychology Club of New York*, 21 (December 1959), 8-12.

Fontenrose, Joseph. *Western Humanities Review*, 23 (Spring 1969), 172-173.

Frye, Northrop. *New York Times Herald Tribune Book Week*, 1 (March 22, 1964), 6, 19.

Gentry, Curt. *San Francisco Sunday Chronicle's This World* (November 15, 1959), 35.

_____. *San Francisco Sunday Chronicle's This World* (May 13, 1962), 38.

Girdler, Lew. *Journal of American Folklore*, 82 (April-June 1969), 171-172.

Gorer, Geoffrey. *Listener*, 63 (June 30, 1960), 1145-1146.

_____. *Listener*, 68 (December 27, 1962), 1101-1102.

Hathorn, Richmond Y. *Classical Journal*, 60 (January 1965), 182-183.

Henderson, Joseph L. *Journal of Analytical Psychology*, 14 (July 1969), 193-194.

James, E. O. *Hibbert Journal*, 58 (July 1960), 415-416.

Jameson, Michael H. *Archaeology*, 18 (Winter 1965), 313.

Kermode, Frank. *Spectator*, No. 6875, 204 (April 1, 1960), 477-478.

Leis, Philip E. *Western Folklore*, 20 (July 1961), 217-220.

Long, Charles H. "Religion and Mythology: A Critical Review of Some Recent Discussions." *History of Religions*, 1 (Winter 1962), 322-331. On Campbell: 325-331.

Martin, David. *Times (of London) Educational Supplement*, No. 3489 (May 13, 1983), 54.

Nottingham, Elizabeth K. *Journal for the Scientific Study of Religion*, 4 (Fall 1964), 113-115.

Nyenhuis, Jacob E. *Classical World*, 58 (October 1964), 50-51.

Opler, Morris E. *New York Herald Tribune Weekly Book Review*, 36 (November 22, 1959), 5.

_____. *Journal of American Folklore*, 75 (January-March 1962), 82-83.

Rieff, Philip. *American Sociological Review*, 25 (December 1960), 975-976.

Robertson, Priscilla. *Progressive*, 33 (February 1969), 50-51.

Skeels, Dell R. *Journal of American Folklore*, 78 (January-March 1965), 71-72.

Sostrom, Shirley. *Journal of Human Relations*, 17 (First Quarter 1969), 155-157.

Sundel, Alfred. *Village Voice* (August 1, 1968), 7, 12.

_____. "Joseph Campbell's Quest for the Grail." *Sewanee Review*, 78 (January-March 1970), 211-216.

Sykes, Gerald. *New York Times Magazine* (May 18, 1969), 6, 22.

S., F. J. *Personalist*, 45 (Autumn 1964), 590-591.

Tabor, Edward O., Jr. *Anglican Theological Review*, 42 (January 1960), 73-74.

Thompson, Josiah. *Review of Metaphysics*, 22 (March 1969), 565.

Watts, Alan W. *Saturday Review*, 45 (June 2, 1962), 36-37.

_____. *New Republic*, 150 (June 27, 1964), 24, 26.

Wilson, Bryan. *New Society*, 26 (November 29, 1973), 544-545.

Worsley, Peter. *Manchester Guardian,* No. 35374 (March 25, 1960), 9.

Reviews of *The Flight of the Wild Gander:*

Ackerman, Robert. *Commentary,* 48 (December 1969), 108-110.
Brandon, S. G. F. *New York Review of Books,* 14 (May 7, 1970), 42-43.
Fontenrose, Joseph. *Western Humanities Review,* 24 (Winter 1970), 86-88.
Greenway, John. *American Anthropologist,* 72 (August 1970), 864-865.
Janeway, Elizabeth. *Christian Science Monitor,* No. 267, 61 (October 9, 1969),
   12.

Reviews of *Myths to Live By:*

Appleyard, J. A. *Commonweal,* 96 (September 29, 1972), 528-530.
Balter, Leon. *Psychoanalytic Quarterly,* 44 (January 1975), 157-163.
Creighton, Peden. *Journal of Religious Thought,* 30 (1973), 64-68.
Laut, Stephen J. *Best Sellers,* 32 (July 1, 1972), 164.
Wilson, Bryan. *New Society,* 26 (November 29, 1973), 544-545.
Wilson, Emmett, Jr. *Saturday Review,* 55 (June 24, 1972), 68.

Reviews of *The Mythic Image:*

Beres, David. *Psychoanalytic Quarterly,* 47 (January 1978), 134-136.
Clifford, Richard J. *Bulletin of the American Schools of Oriental Research,* No.
   223 (October 1976), 75-76.
Cully, Iris V. *Review of Books and Religion,* 4 (1975), 11.
Dick, Bernard F. *Books Abroad,* 49 (Autumn 1975), 861-862.
Ditsky, John. *Southern Humanities Review,* 11 (Summer 1977), 321-322.
Doty, William. *Parabola,* 1 (Winter 1976), 99-103.
Frank, Luanne. *Thought,* 51 (December 1976), 450-451.
Friedman, Albert B. *Western Folklore,* 35 (January 1976), 80-82.
Fuller, Edmund. *Wall Street Journal,* 185 (May 12, 1975), 12.
Gardner, John. *New York Times Book Review* (December 28, 1975), 15-16.
Green, Peter. *Washington Post Book World* (April 20, 1975), 4.
Henderson, Joseph. *Quadrant,* 8 (Summer 1975), 69-70.
Hoffman, Ruth. *Journal of Analytical Psychology,* 22 (July 1977), 279-281.
Kerrigan, William. "The Raw, The Cooked and the Half-Baked." *Virginia
   Quarterly Review,* 51 (Autumn 1975), 646-656.
Long, Charles H. "The Dreams of Professor Campbell: Joseph Campbell's *The
   Mythic Image.*" *Religious Studies Review,* 6 (October 1980), 261-271.
Prescott, Peter S. *Newsweek,* 85 (March 31, 1975), 75-76.
Prigent, P. *Revue d'Histoire et de Philosophie Religieuses,* 63 (October-December
   1983), 510.
Reardon, Patrick Henry. *Review for Religious,* 34 (July 1975), 634.
Robbins, Michael D. *American Journal of Psychiatry,* 133 (September 1976),
   1098.

Sargeant, Winthrop. *New Yorker,* 51 (July 21, 1975), 86-88.
Shea, Glenn J. *American Book Collector,* 26 (July-August 1976), 2, 4.
Tissot, Georges. *Sciences Religieuses,* 6 (1976-77), 568-571.
Vickery, John B. *Sewanee Review,* 84 (Spring 1976), lvi-lix.

Reviews of *Historical Atlas of World Mythology,* vol. I

Brand, Stewart. *CoEvolution Quarterly* (Spring 1984), 108.
Brown, Michael F. *Smithsonian,* 14 (February 1984), 150-153.
Hart, Jeffrey. *National Review,* 36 (July 13, 1984), 45-47.
Highwater, Jamake. *Commonweal,* 112 (March 25, 1985), 183, 187-188.
Hirsch, Marina. *San Francisco Sunday Chronicle Book Review* (December 4,
    1983), 1, 18.
Leeming, David. *Parabola,* 9 (January 1984), 90-92.
Leroux, Charles. *Chicago Tribune* (January 19, 1984), Section 5, 1, 3.
Meyer, Alfred. *Science '84,* 5 (May 1984), 90.
Nader, Laura. *Los Angeles Times Book Review* (December 11, 1983), 3.
O'Flaherty, Wendy. *New York Times Book Review* (December 18, 1983), 3, 24.
Pfeiffer, John E. *Nature,* 308 (April 26, 1984), 796.
Sargeant, Winthrop. *New Yorker,* 59 (February 13, 1984), 126-128.
Segal, Robert A. *Journal for the Scientific Study of Religion,* 24 (June 1985), 232-
    234.

(b) ARTICLES AND OTHER DISCUSSIONS

Beattie, Paul H. "A Perspective on Mythology." *Religious Humanism,* 17 (Autumn
    1983), 173-181. On Campbell: 179.
Bennetts, Leslie. "A Master of Mythology Is Honored." *New York Times,* 134
    (March 1, 1985), Section C, 4.
Chase, Richard. *Democratic Vista.* Garden City, NY: Doubleday Anchor Books,
    1958. On Campbell: 74-86.
_____. "Myth as Literature." *English Institute Essays 1947.* New York: Columbia
    University Press, 1948. Pp. 3-22. On Campbell: 7.
Clarke, Gerald. "The Need for New Myths." Essay. *Time,* 99 (January 17, 1972),
    50-51.
D'Arcy, M. C. "God and Mythology." *Heythrop Journal,* 1 (April 1960), 91-104.
    On Campbell: 95-104.
De Laszlo, Violet. "The Goal in Jungian Psychotherapy." *Spring* (1952), 59-75.
    On Campbell: 68-69.
Dorson, Richard M. "Mythology and Folklore." *Annual Review of Anthropology,*
    2 (1973), 107-126. On Campbell: 107-108.
Doty, William G. *Mythography.* Tuscaloosa: University of Alabama Press, 1986.
    On Campbell: 52-55, 108-110, 121, 124-125, 176-178.
Dundes, Alan. *Interpreting Folklore.* Bloomington: Indiana University Press,
    1960. On Campbell: 224-225, 231-232.

Jewett, Robert, and John Shelton Lawrence. *The American Monomyth.* Garden City, NY: Doubleday Anchor Books, 1977. On Campbell: xix-xx, 249.

Miller, David L. *"Homo Religiosus* and the Death of God." *Journal of Bible and Religion*, 34 (October 1966), 305-315. On Campbell: 306-309.

Perry, John Weir. "The Messianic Hero." *Journal of Analytical Psychology*, 17 (July 1972), 184-198. On Campbell: 185.

Sandler, Florence, and Darrell Reeck. "The Masks of Joseph Campbell." *Religion*, 11 (January 1981), 1-20.

Segal, Robert A. "Joseph Campbell's Theory of Myth: An Essay Review of His *Oeuvre.*" *Journal of the American Academy of Religion*, Supplement, 44 (March 1978), 98-114.

Sharpe, Eric J. *Comparative Religion: A History.* New York: Scribner's, 1975. On Campbell: 212-213.

Zemljanova, L. "The Struggle between the Reactionary and the Progressive Forces in Contemporary American Folkloristics." *Journal of the Folklore Institute*, 1 (1964), 130-144. On Campbell: 132.

(c) APPLICATIONS

Anonymous. *"Beowulf,* Mythology and Ritual: A Common-reader Exploration." *Xavier University Studies*, 3 (June 1964), 89-102.

Hansen, Terry L. "Myth-Adventure in Leigh Brackett's 'Enchantress of Venus'." *Extrapolation*, 23 (Spring 1982), 77-82.

James, William C. "The Canoe Trip as Religious Quest." *Studies in Religion*, 10 (Spring 1981), 151-166.

Kaempchen, Martin. "Stages of Development in a Holy Life." *Journal of Dharma*, 8 (April-June 1983), 127-146.

Prats, A. J. "The Individual, the World, and the Life of Myth in *Fellini Satyricon.*" *South Atlantic Bulletin*, 44 (1979), 45-58.

Tomasulo, Frank P. "Mr. Jones Goes to Washington: Myth and Religion in *Raiders of the Lost Ark.*" *Quarterly Review of Film Studies*, 7 (Fall 1982), 331-340.

Williams, Anne. "Browning's 'Childe Roland,' Apprentice for Night." *Victorian Poetry*, 21 (Spring 1983), 27-42.

Winchell, Mark Royden. "Bellow's Hero with a Thousand Faces: The Use of Folk Myth in *Henderson the Rain King.*" *Mississippi Folk Register*, 14 (1981), 115-126.